THE STREET LEGENDS SERIES
FROM SETH FERRANTI AND GORILLA CONVICT

STREET LEGENDS VOL. 6

"THE MOST POTENT VOICE OF THE STREETS."

Crack, Rap and Murder:

The Cocaine Dreams of Alpo and Rich Porter

Hip-Hop Folklore from the Streets of Harlem

SETH FERRANTI

ISBN 978-0-9889760-3-0

Printed in the United States of America

First Printing

Book Design by Matt Pramschufer
www.pramschufer.com

Gorilla Convict Publications
www.gorillaconvict.com

To order additional copies of Rap, Crack and Murder visit
www.gorillaconvict.com

ISBN 978-0-9889760-3-0

PRAISE FOR SETH FERRANTI

"During the past decade, Seth Ferranti has become a master story teller, historian and chronicler of the street legends largely spawned by drug prohibition." Ron Chepesiuk, author of Escobar vs Cali and Sergeant Smack

"In his new book, Ferranti has, from behind bars, published his masterpiece, an amazing study of one brutal and vicious but legendary gang's dominance of the crack trade during a new era in the history of the black gangster where art and the streets intersected to shape the growing hip-hop culture." amazon.com

"If you like gangster stories, true crime, hip-hop or New York culture, this is a great read. I will definitely be reading more of Seth Ferranti's work and I have to say more authors like him are needed. He's already a force, but once he's released I believed we will go from seeing his name on pages to in credits. Hopefully on an unfiltered HBO type of series." Mobb Bunny23, amazon.com

"Another great book from Seth Ferranti with page turning, raw uncut details about some of the coldest crews and cats out there. Highly recommended to anyone that is into books about true crime." Kindle Edition, amazon.com

"This is not sensationalized writing about what goes on in the streets but very well written and researched journalism that goes in-depth into the genesis and environments that created these men. If you want to know what the streets of urban American produce, I suggest you read this book."

Black TK, Larceny Media

"Seth Ferranti is the real deal. His books are serious. They tell the sides of things you don't see in the movies. The bad side of gangster life and what it involves as well as the good. This book is a must read for anyone who likes this genre of books." amazon.com

"Ferranti writes like the gangsters speak. His books give a voice that is far different than just a historical recitation. Really well done work for fans of street level true crime." Scott M. Deitche, author of Rogue Mobster

"Take a ride with Seth Ferranti as he gathers knowledge from interviews, testimonials of how and why these young men become the epitome of their city. This book profiles each legend during the crack epidemic and how each one is on one accord with the no snitching movement during their reign in the streets." Readers Paradise Book Club

"I remember watching New Jack City as a kid and feeling like it was a fantasy similar to Avatar or Alice in Wonderland, thinking no gang could be as ruthless, as determined, and as exciting as the CMB. Truth be told, I think the exploits of Fat Cat and his crew far upstage any fictionalized account that could be conceived in Hollywood. The book digs into the origin and really gives you a look into the mind of the drug lords more so than watching American Gangster or listening to a few rap songs." amazon.com

"Seth creates the perfect balance of admiration and consequences for these street legends. The moral of the story is that crime does not pay, but it does make for one hell of a read." The Pen

"It is a war report live and direct from behind enemy lines. Raw and uncut. I recommend this to anyone who is looking to get more knowledge on American gangsters and how they operate." amazon.com

"Seth Ferranti brings clarity to the chaos and pulls you in with him showing the allegiances, hierarchies and threats that exist in the streets. I was gripped and you should read this." amazon.com

"The sheer violence and brutality of the book exposes the reader to the harsh environment that exists within the inner-cities and is an alarming wake up call to the kill or be killed mentality that exists." barnesandnoble.com

This book is dedicated to all those who supported me and my work while I was striving to come up from inside the belly of the beast. Thank you.

INTRO

In the mid-80s, there was no P. Diddy or Jay Z on MTV or BET setting trends and letting the people know what was hot. There was only the streets, and the denizens of the block that created chaos on those streets. Their lives weren't televised to the mainstream, but they dictated who was on, what car was en vogue and what jewelry to rock. They had the swagger and confidence of a Mafia don. They were the shot callers and the dudes that made things jump. There were no rappers in a music video for young brothers to mimic and emulate. There was only the streets and the gun thugs and dealers that held court. Their styles became fashion and their exploits iconic.

Back in the day, it was the drug lords who were setting the scene. By creating their own superstar images and status, they made underworld history. The young drug thugs swagger-jacked the spirit of hip-hop and made it their own. With the boldness and brashness of a stateside Don Dada, the young hip-hop hustlers who cultivated the New York drug game during the Ronald Reagan years, set the tone for the lifestyles of the ghetto rich and famous. The lives and deaths of the notorious gangsters, plying their illicit trade, captivated the inner-city's imagination like none before them. They were the live and in your face music video or Hollywood movie, and their film was going down frame by frame in the streets.

In Harlem, a story that contained all the ingredients of a good gangster flick- drugs, sex, murder, action, lust, envy, greed, hatred and betrayal, took place. The starring roles went to two young hustlers in pursuit of the American dream, who lived and died by the code of the streets. They became major players in the New York City drug trade by the ages of 16 and 17, making street and crime lord history in the historic black Mecca that was setting trends for the world.

The duo were icons of high style and luxury, and influenced the origins of rap, street culture and hip-hop in the Harlem landscapes of the mid-80s. More so than many others, their infamy and folklore, has stayed relevant in rap music and entertainment. The stories of these two cocaine legends represent a true life testimony to the paths one can take in the drug game. Despite the glorification of the life, only three outcomes are a reality- prison, hell or death. And these two Harlem street stars found out the hard way as they pursued their cocaine dreams. Their names were Alpo and Rich Porter.

From the ages of 14 to 25, Alpo and Rich Porter mesmerized the streets of New York, by creating tantalizing trends and daring exploits that left their contemporaries in the drug game looking pale in comparison. They were the flashiest and most daring gangsters Uptown had ever seen and the impact they made on the streets of Harlem during their short reign have proved monumental in popular culture. Alpo and Rich Porter, even today, remain lightning rods for controversy and enigmas of the highest order.Romanticized as much as they are vilified. And Alpo has epitomized the love/hate relationship the streets have for the pair.

The admiration and distaste he has elicited, in various degrees and from all angles, has enabled their legends to grow and live on. To Alpo, it was always business and never personal. And this maxim held true when he killed his partner, Rich Porter. The murder of his best friend has been remembered in the chronicles of gangster lore as one of the most treacherous acts ever committed and been immortalized in hip-hop lore. This story represents the cocaine dreams of Alpo and Rich Porter and how they ended in tragedy for all concerned. But despite the outcome, their legends are still celebrated.

CHAPTER 1

THE BEGINNING

"On the back of the bike with Alpo/doin' a back down one0two-three/hopin' to stay alive/favorite spot, Rooftop"- LL Cool J

Alberto "Alpo" Martinez was from East Rivers projects in Spanish Harlem, better known as the Eastside. "Alpo's building was on 105th and First Avenue," the Spanish Harlem hustler says. "Alpo was Puerto Rican, not Dominican. Very few people knew that because of his complexion and his swagger. Those who grew up with him in the area knew. He used to hang out in Wilson projects which were across the street. His childhood was good."

It's said Alpo never met his father and that he spent summers away from Harlem as a child at Fresh Air Fund camps. "Po always stood out. He went to camp. His mom was always taking him out. He was a dark skinned Puerto Rican. I called him negro. He spoke Spanish real well." The Spanish Harlem hustler says.

"I can't picture anyone not liking Alpo." He continues. The nigga's smile embraced everyone. Going to the Boys Club, he wanted to be a Marine, a cadet." A nice white family involved in the Fresh Air Fun camps took a liking to Alpo and after the summer program was over they would send for him. This family grew to love him. They wanted to adopt him, but it wasn't meant to be. Life had another fate for Alpo.

Alpo grew up in a single parent household, along with his three siblings. He had an older sister, a younger sister Monica, an older brother, who he had no real relations with because he was literally crazy, and his mom whom he loved dearly. "I have a wonderful mother, very strong Hispanic mother," Alpo said.

The neighborhood was mostly black and Puerto Rican, with a few white families still living in East Rivers and the surrounding projects- Wilson, New Metro North and Old Metro North. New Metro ran from 100th Street and 1st Avenue to 102nd Street and F.D.R. East River ran from 102nd and 105th Street to 1st Avenue and F.D.R. Old Metro North ran from 101st Street and 102nd Street to 1st and 2nd Avenues. Then Wilson completed the square, running from 105th and 106th Street to 1st Avenue and F.D.R. That equated to four projects in the middle of Spanish Harlem, running the span of six New York City blocks. A lot was happening in that small area and Alpo was usually in the middle of it.

East River was the biggest of the four projects with a total of 29 buildings. Twenty-three of those buildings were six story buildings with five apartments on each floor. There were six bigger buildings that were 15 stories high, with eight apartments on each floor. It was said that East River projects was a world of its own.

"From as far as I can remember Alpo lived in East River projects, because his sister Monica used to be a cheerleader on our Pee Wee and little league baseball team." The East River boriqua says. "His older brother Flaco was a straight nut case. Completely crazy, mental hospital type crazy. He used to freak out and go wild. They accused Flaco of trying to kill or rape some chick when he was young.

"There was always something going on in the hood, like

block parties or whatever. The big park in the back of East Rivers, as well as the basketball court were the official jam spots, where DJ Dollar Bill from Wilson projects would set up shop with his equipment- two turn tables, big ass speakers and 100 extension cords hanging out of someone's apartment window giving them juice to jam. The neighborhood was a melting pot, because we had black, white and Spanish and everyone else that had to come live there, because you weren't there because you wanted to be there."

Alpo went to PS5382 in the Bronx, from elementary school up to the sixth grade on the Eastside, then he attended St. Lucy's Catholic school and went to Automotive Mechanical High School in Brooklyn for a minute. Jay-Z went there too. Alpo also attended Julia Richmond High School. But school wasn't where he would make his name at.He had a serious jones for the streets.

"I have no idea about how he got the name Alpo," the East River boriqua says. "I just know they called him that as far back as I can remember. That nigga went to one of those schools for troublemakers or kids who caught cases. He was a dusty kid, you know, nothing special, but not many from the hood were above the dusty level." In New York's Spanish Harlem it was a hard life and Alpo did whatever he could to stand out.

"He was like 140, a little scrappy dude, liked to pay attention. As he got older, he started filling out." The Spanish Harlem hustler says. "He took sparring and boxing lessons with Wilfredo Benitiz, but the pull of the streets was too much. Like any other kid, Alpo didn't want to depend on his mother. He had the eye of the tiger. Po had it, like Lebron and MJ." Alpo had street dreams and unlike others he had the heart to make them come true.

"There was definitely the Latin vibe big time in the neighborhood," the East River boriqua says. "It was Spanish Harlem when you hit the street, you knew that the name went perfect with the place. It was the type of neighborhood where everyone knew each other. Where the local grocery store, Julios, let people take credit until the welfare check came or you got paid on Fridays.

"Some families were dirt poor and others just a notch above them, so when you're living that kind of life day in and day out in the Mecca of the World, Manhattan, everybody wants to shine, everybody wants to rise to the ghetto superstar status. But wanting is one thing and actually going out there and making it happen is a whole other story.

"This motherfucker Alpo used to ride around the neighborhood on a ten speed doing wheelies with a mouth full of beans and a big ass straw from McDonald's shooting everyone as he rode by with beans. Dudes wanted to be friends with him because he was always into something and kids in the neighborhood knew that people respected and somewhat feared him because he would go at it with anyone."

As a child he robbed people and snatched pocket books. Alpo was in the life early, already in the mix by the time he was 13 or 14 years old. He was born in 1966, so by 1980 he was getting his. He had a knack for getting people to like him and he was always scheming on ways to make money. Alpo had no fear and that was attractive to older criminals.

"I had a friend on 105th that took me under his wing." Alpo said. Alpo started as a runner. A certain O.G. had him on the corner. Alpo was the first one out on the block; it'd be early in the morning and cold as hell. Alpo was maybe 13, he was young, but he was on the street grinding. He was really street smart for such a young dude. He used to hang out on Amsterdam selling heroin packets.

"The hustle was big in Harlem and back then dope was king. Coke was second, because crack hadn't hit the streets yet. Weed was everyone's bread drug." The East River boriqua says. "The local drug dealer respected everyone that lived in the buildings they hustled in front of and everyone respected him all the same. There were enemies like everywhere else, but there were some unwritten rules in the projects back then, that I'm sure don't exist now.

"Like if you were a straight arrow dude, that didn't agree with what was going on in front of your building, you didn't call the cops to address the issue, you simply addressed the issue. That's one thing about the projects, you could never underestimate the next man, because the projects were tough and there was always someone tougher than you wanting to make a name for himself.

"But even with all that, it was a beautiful place to grow up. When fights broke out between kids their whole family got it on- sisters with sisters, younger brothers with younger brothers, fathers with fathers- that was the unity that you saw in the hood." Life wasn't easy in Spanish Harlem, families stuck together.

"We knew Alpo personally, before anyone who isn't from East River did. We are from the same projects as he is and witnessed firsthand what others from New York didn't know. Before there was a Wayne Perry, there was a Randy Love who terrified the shit out of a lot of dudes in Harlem and New York period," the Spanish Harlem hustler says. Randy Love was the friend and O.G. that took Alpo on and put him under his wing.

"Randy Love was from across the street on 105th Street and 1st Ave, Wilson projects. Randy terrorized the shit out of all of Harlem. He was a gangster that was vicious before anybody ever heard of a Wayne Perry. His reputation was that he was not to be fucked with. He was a killer and niggas knew what time it was." The Spanish Harlem hustler says.

"Randy Love used to steal Greyhound buses from the Port Authority for fun and bring them back around the way. He used to put Alpo up to running into spots and staking out the joint, then they'd come back and rob the shit out of the Dominicans. Randy Love took Alpo under his wing, but he was mostly gone a lot, because he stayed on Rikers Island.

"I think Randy was the one who probably made him even tougher, because we all knew he was tough, but when he was starting to run with Randy, everybody knew that he was taking it to the next level. There were rumors that they were sticking up drug dealers and they robbed and killed a cash carrier that used to pick up the cash on a 112th Street dope spot. That cash belonged to the dudes from the lower Eastside and this led to a body being dropped damn near everyday in the hood." Randy Love taught Alpo a lot about the streets, but Alpo was gaining other skills that would help him also.

"I was learning to drive. I was a good driver too. I was wild, things of that nature." Alpo said. "I was known for my driving. The first car I bought with my own money was a four door 77 Chevy Malibu. I put some music in it, turned the headers around and that was my joint. The car that really put me on the map was a Toyota Corolla. I used to drive crazy in it. I really thought it was a racecar.

"It was a blue five speed with fat wheels and a system in it. I'm talking 1981-82. I was still in Julia Richmond high school at the time. I thought I was the man. I crashed it. I didn't hit anybody so I jumped out the joint and just left the car. I jumped in a cab and got out of there. I loved that car. I used to be at the Rooftop with that joint on the sidewalk, like it was a BMW.

"I remember I got my first BMW out of 115th. That's when the 318 was out. I got it from a crackhead who smoked so much in my spot he had to give it to me to pay off his crack debt. It was a blue joint, with a sunroof and light gray seats. His family didn't know he was getting high and he smoked like 10 grand in my spot. His family ended up paying me some of the money and I let it go." The young Alpo was a gangster in training, a young reckless dude who didn't give a fuck.

"Our everyday environment is what set the ground work for him to want to shine." The East River boriqua says. "We all seen what the dope boys and coke stars had and how they made life in the projects look like they were living in a penthouse on 63rd Street and Central Park West overlooking the park. Everybody wanted that, Alpo just pushed toward it more. If I'm right, he came from a single parent home, just his mom. In that home he had one crazy ass brother and a younger sister. I'm sure the thoughts were for him to get some cash and get out of there so he could have his own place.

"The way that welfare apartments work is that the boys room together, so he probably had crazy ass Flaco sleeping in the room with him. Monica probably had her own room and the mom her own room. So here you are living tight as a motherfucker in the hood on 105th Street, one block from a good dope spot on 105th and 1st and 2nd Avenue.

"You damn near taste the money that is being made up the block, not to mention that we weren't far from the upper middle class whites that lived good in Manhattan. Ninety-sixth Street was like the unofficial border of the dirt poor to middle and upper class America so we were just nine blocks away from what felt like a world away in lifestyles." Alpo's involvement with Randy Love led him into the stick up game and he was a natural gun thug.

"We started robbing the Dominicans together." Alpo said. "We did stick ups. I remember when the Dominicans used to have weight up in their apartments on scales. We would rob them just for that. Because I looked so young they would just open the door. I would go in first, survey the area, and since I spoke Spanish, I would understand what they were talking about. After that, I'd tell my man the layout, where the guns were. Then we would go back.

"We were robbing them. The takes were good back then; we'd get $10 to 15 grand and half a kilo in cocaine. After the stick ups stopped we started selling dope for some big names. Then we branched off. My partner was always in and out of jail." With Randy Love at his side, Alpo had the whole Eastside on lockdown. Dudes were shook. "He had a posse. He blew up at 15. Wore the big gold chains at age 15. From Randy Love, he learned how ruthless he had to be. He had the stick up kids in check. He worked older men. They listened and respected him." The Spanish Harlem hustler says. "They bodied whoever the fuck got in their way. Randy Love is serving life in the state now, but back then he scared the shit out of these niggas and he and Alpo caught mad bodies together for years before Alpo met Rich Porter."

In the streets people think Rich Porter made Alpo, but he was big and in charge of the Eastside before he even went to Uptown or the Westside. That was just Alpo branching off. His feet were firmly entrenched in the drug game and criminal underworld. His name was already ringing in the streets. But Alpo wanted a bigger stage.

"He started doing stick ups around the outskirts of the neighborhood. He was nice on bikes that he rode and used to stick up white boys in Central Park and right over the border in Manhattan." The East River boriqua says. "He did a juvi bid and when he came back he put on some fly shit. Back then the BVD's were the flashiest shit out. The tank tops, t-shirts, LaCross, Adidas, Pumas and Herring Bone chains. He was getting what he wanted because that's what stick up kids do.

"He was sticking up kids for Cannondales and Mongoose bikes that were $500 to $1,000 back in the 80s and selling them in the hood for $100 to 200 bucks. This is where he started getting right with his gear, so the flashiness was there even when he was young. This is where him and Randy Love probably got to know each other. Randy was from Wilson, right across the street from Alpo's building and a dude with a serious rep for going in a putting in work.

"He was a stickup kid by all means that pushed niggas shit back in a heartbeat. They were a good fit because neither one of them were afraid to get theirs and Randy got him by a couple of years. Randy is up in Greenhaven doing a life bid." From his prison cell, Randy Love would feed Alpo hookups.

"During one stay he had a partner with him upstate that stepped to him," Alpo said. "He told my partner he needed some bodyguards. His friend had a Dominican connect who liked dealing with blacks and had a job or two as bodyguards. That's how I really came to the Westside, this guy on 129th and Broadway. We were introduced to the Dominican and became his bodyguards. My man's man told him that we were wild and if he had any problems we'd take care of it for him. That's when we started dealing with heavy coke. This Dominican kid was strong.

"We went on a few missions stepping to people about his money. My partner was wild and couldn't control himself so he got locked up and went to jail again. That left me with the Dominican kid alone. When he found out I was Puerto Rican he liked it. This way he was able to put me in a room with Puerto Rican and Dominican customers who thought I was black. These customers would talk freely around me about jerking the Dominican, thinking I didn't understand them. Later, I would tell him what they were saying and we would handle the situation.

"All that boosted my position. When one of the guys that picked up coke for the Dominican got caught stealing I got his position. Now I was going to get the kilos and dealing with the customers. I started dipping into the coke. He never knew it was missing." As Alpo got himself in position and Randy Love got a life sentence their once promising relation deteriorated.

"As for Alpo's relationship with Randy they were close, but not homeboys 'til the end," the East River boriqua says. "When Randy went to jail they said that Alpo was fucking his baby moms, a very pretty, light skin black girl with light eyes and a beautiful body from Wilson projects. Everyone was talking about how they would kill one another if Randy came out of jail." It was the first of many betrayals for Alpo, a trait that would come to define him.

With Randy Love out of the picture and plenty of enemies in Spanish Harlem, Alpo made the move that would certify his legend. He started hanging out and doing business in Uptown. "I remember before I even came to the Westside, it was all about Rich and L.A." Alpo said. "I went down to 116th Street, between 7th and 8th Avenue. There was a good dude down there who had some dope called Tiger Paw. I met these cats and they had the dough. I asked them if I could get down and they let me put nickel bottles of coke down there. I was selling about 300 to 500 bottles. The money was free and the dude that ran the block was like, 'The coke is your thing, the dope is ours.' So it was nice for a minute. They saw me as a young wild kid and someway, somehow I got connected with them. "They rode motorcycles and I loved riding. I would dog the bikes and do 20 block long wheelies. I enjoyed riding bikes and I was definitely one of the guys that got busy and people enjoyed watching. I went back to 115th Street. The people I met when I was selling the base coke started getting hit with crack. So they started hitting me off on 115th Street. Now I'm not only getting it from the Dominican, I'm getting it from everybody. Like I said earlier, I was stealing from my man. I had this free coke and I was driving my man's car. Dudes thought I was blowing up." To the streets, Alpo was the man, even if he was fronting, he played the part.

"His name was always ringing in our neighborhood, so to people from the projects it wasn't a surprise when he started blowing up," the East River boriqua says. "It was probably more of a surprise how big the nigga blew up and how he went being known in the hood to being known in the state and others. This was in the 80s and Alpo was a monster on a motorcycle, doing wheelies for damn near two city blocks, wearing the famous German helmet. That nigga bust his ass one time on 1st Avenue and was twisted. He got up, put the motorcycle on the sidewalk and just left in a car, leaving the bike like trash."

"That base shit is taking over," Alpo said. "Niggas is getting rich with that shit. You alls lil' man came over here yesterday talking about wanting to open up shop over here with that shit. Lil' GQ nigga. What's that lil' niggas name?" They told him Darryl. "Yeah, shorty from Uptown. I had to tell shorty, nah, you can't do nothing in this block."

Alpo pulled out five small glass vials filled with crack. "Which one of you bad niggas want to be the first to take a hit of this shit?" Everyone declined, they followed the hustlers creed, don't get high on your own supply, but Alpo didn't give a fuck. "I was just bullshitting you all to see who was gonna be the first nigga to suck the glass dick."

Alpo started dating this older known hustler's girl called

Mousy. She had a burgundy Mercedes Benz 190 and a Subaru, and she started letting Alpo drive them. "On a Rooftop night I'd get the 190 and front," Alpo said. "Everybody thought I was really getting it now. I was driving both her joints. A lot of older cats wanted her, so this gave me more status. Not only with the fellas, but with the females too. She let me hold her boyfriend's jewelry. He was in jail, so I used to wear all his chains and front. I met a crew at the Rooftop, they hit me off and I took that back down to 115th Street. Everybody was getting paid."

As Alpo became a name in his own right he was still in the shadow of Harlem's native son and street superstar, Rich Porter. Back then when Alpo was establishing himself in Uptown, Rich Porter was the man. Barely 16-years-old himself, Rich Porter was the epitome of gangster coolness and a hip-hop hustler for the ages. Little did Alpo know that he would skyrocket to street fame as Rich Porter's partner.

Richard Porter was born in 1965 and began his rise in the drug game at 12-years-old. "Me and Rich went to school together," another drug dealer of repute, Azie "AZ" Faison said. "He lived up the block from me, we grew up together. When I was working in the cleaners across the street from where he lived, Rich used to hustle on Amsterdam Avenue and 145th Street. Rich wasn't selling what you would call real drugs at the time. He used to sell some shit to the white boys.

"I don't know where he learned it and he never told me, but that shit used to work. He used to go to the supermarket and get a seasoning called sage and some eggs and take all the sage and put it in a bowl and then crack the eggs, mix it, put it in the oven and let it cook. Then the shit would get hard and he'd take it out and mash it down flat. Once it dried, it looked and smelled exactly like hash. White boys used to come from Jersey and Rich used to sell them pieces for like twenty, fifty dollars. He used to stay fresh like that, sheepskins and leather bombers."

Rich Porter always kept a new pair of sneakers on his feet. His favorites were the white on white Reebok Classics. Rich would wear Bally sneakers also and shop at all the trendy stores- Apple Town, Jew Man and KP Kongs. Being fresh and in style was important to Rich and he had big dreams. In New York at that time the Colombians were bringing in massive amounts of cocaine. It was a cocaine explosion. The Dominicans had it and they needed someone to move it and they used the blacks.

Every young hustler back then had a BMW or Mercedes Benz book in his pocket. They would talk about which one they were going to get. They would watch the older players in the street stunt and drive through the hood in their Beamers and Benz, trying to identify what make and model they were from the book. When Rich saw the dudes cruise through, he would tell his friends, "One day I'm gonna cop one of them joints." Rich was on his way to making a lot of money.

"At 12 was when the drug game started coming in." Patricia Porter, Rich's sister said. "He knew how to master a hustle. My little brother was 12-years-old and chose to sell marijuana. We knew what drugs were early on. We came up in that world." Rich was getting his feet wet in the game, but he would make his mark in Harlem with a kid named Donald "LA" Johnson.

"There was a guy named LA," AZ said. "Who pioneered it all." One hundred forty fourth street was LA's block. LA had the dope stamped Mad Monkey. "Rich came on the scene and LA was getting it." The Harlem gangster says. "Rich was from Martha Hill and Amsterdam. LA brought him down on the Avenue to get that heron money. LA taught Rich a lot about the drug game."

LA also taught Rich about being a gangster. LA would fight and pull out a pistol in a minute, but most of the time dudes would back down out of respect. In the streets, everyone would be tested. It was a rite of passage.

"Rich started selling dope with LA on 144th Street." AZ said. The two young hustlers quickly became the stars of Uptown. LA and Rich made their monumental mark when they rode through Harlem on a two thousand dollar, two seat Schwinn bicycle, with a boom box strapped to the back playing Tee-Ski

Valleys hit single, Catch the Beat. That was when the streets of Harlem took notice.

Rich was wearing an all white Yankee jacket with matching hat and red and white Nike Cortez leather track sneakers, the dopeman shoes. LA wore a similar outfit, but in dark blue and his sneakers had blue leather instead of red. The way they looked made a statement. They became celebrities in the hood. Trap stars of the day. They were the first to rock baseball jackets. LA and Rich were too fly and in the streets of Harlem their styles were admired and copied. Even future rap superstars jacked their swagger.

"I used to make sure my gear was correct," LL Cool J said. "Even before I made a record, I dressed the part- Sergio Valente or colored Lee jeans, the shell top Adidas or Pumas, Le Tigre jackets and of course, the Kangols. I even had a pair of Gazelles. We would snatch the leather bombers and sheepskin coats."

In Uptown, on 144th Street between 7th and Lenox Avenues, young LA and Rich continued to make their marks on the streets of Harlem. They started out with the Peugeot ten speeds, then got the Champ mopeds and finally the dirt bikes like the Yamaha YZ's. Rich and LA put on shows with the dirt bikes doing wheelies, doughnuts and burnouts up and down 7th and Lenox Avenues. In that way they were similar to Alpo, before they even met him.

Police chased them, as people on the side walks cheered them on. They attracted a lot of followers and admirers. Little Darryl Barnes, who people said was Nicky Barnes son, was LA and Rich's best friend and right hand man. "There was LA, Jason, Rich, Travis, T-Money, John-John, Darryl Barnes, Doo Wop, Fat Dave," the Uptown player says. LA supplied a lot of dudes with coke and him, Darryl, Rich and the others were cool. They would freebase, sniff, smoke and get high. Rich would pull out the pink cocaine, "I guess you all don't want none of this pink shit, so I'm gonna knock this out myself." In the 80s cocaine was en vogue and thought of as the rich man's drug. The young hustlers emulated the rock stars as LA and Rich courted the streets.

"LA had mad girls, he was the talk of the town. They had the dirt bikes, mopeds- if you wasn't a part of their movement you weren't down." AZ said. Dudes on the block would notice the fine girls who flocked around them, but some were off limits. "You see that dress Tracy got on?" They would say. "That shit cost like a G. You see that rock they got on they fingers? Stop playing you think they care about you? Nigga, Tracy is LA's wife and Yolanda is Rich's wife. They living the dream that every female in Harlem want to live."

When Rich and LA would fly by on their dirt bikes, the girls went crazy. "That's my niggas, I bet they jet on the police." Tracy said. "LA and Rich is my babies. They are the two youngest niggas in Harlem getting paid." LL Cool J was down with the dirt bikes too. "All I ever wanted was a dirt bike," LL said. "It seemed every cool kid in the neighborhood had one." The future rap superstar was very influenced by Harlem's street stars.

Rich and LA weren't rappers, they were in the drug game. They moved heroin. They were making serious bank for some teenagers. LA was the first of the young hustlers to purchase a foreign made car with drug money. LA drove through Harlem in an all black turbo Saab with fog lights that were blinding. He rode through Uptown with his man Rich.

"LA had the Saab 900. He was the first dude in Harlem to have a jeep and played the Dollar Bill Y'all song." The Harlem gangster says. "They started the driving with one hand, leaning back." During the early-80s in Harlem, the Saab was the car of choice for young hustlers. Anybody who was getting money wanted one.

"LA was the first young kid around that time who busted out with a new car," AZ said. "He had the Saab 900 Turbo, the year was 86 and the car was an 87. They was down together and they would come to the cleaners and bring mad clothes, cracking jokes like, 'Yo, A, you gotta stop fucking with the cleaners, you gotta get with this.' I saw how they were rolling, they were rolling for real. They had the best clothes and hoes chasing them.

Basically every young kid in town wanted to be like Rich and LA."

A young LA was very popular in Harlem. He was only like 15 years old when he first started getting money in Harlem. On top of that, he was a slick talking, basketball playing gangster, who all the girls thought was real cute. With Rich Porter at his side, they were a magical duo. A Biggie Smalls and Jay-Z, so to speak.

"When he spoke or did anything you wanted to be around," AZ said. "Just to say you were there. He and Rich were young cats, both getting crazy money from dealing heroin in the hood. They were also the first young cats I saw making big paper and flossing the cars and jewelry. LA busted out with the Saab 900 Turbo, it was black on black with white piping and a chrome exhaust pipe.

"Within a month's time, Rich busted out with the black on black BMW 528E. It had the black and white lamb seats. Another hustler from Uptown had the burgundy BMW 535. His man came through with the black Volvo Wagon and another had the Jeep Wagoneer. It was unbelievable. These cats were just out of junior high." At 16, Rich was known for flamboyance and a high profile lifestyle. He could be seen on Harlem's streets showing off his brand new BMW.

"Richard was a man before his time. He was a movement that came from the ashes of the ghetto and transcended into something bigger than life itself." Velma Porter, Rich's mom said. The drug lords had money to spend and didn't mind doing everything first class. Rich and LA would spend about $2,500 a piece preparing to go to the Michael Jackson concert at Madison Square Garden. They flaunted their wealth and status, letting everyone know who they were and what they were about.

"Rich, LA and their man Cee-Moe were driving Rich's brand new BMW. It was a beautiful foreign car that was bound to attract the attention of cops. Sure enough the cops pulled them over. The officers pulled them out of the car and began to search them." AZ said. "Me and other young cats watched from across the street, hoping they didn't get locked up. After questioning them about wearing bulletproof vests, the police let them go. Rich jumped back into his ride like nothing happened. He pulled off blowing his horn as he winked his eye at me.

"To young cats in the hood that was some gangster shit. Minutes later, Sean Mo blew past in the brown 300 ZX t-top. Those were the days when every kid in our hood wanted to be like them, if you didn't, you were considered a sucker, that was the game. The word popular could not begin to describe their status, the spell they cast on everyone was truly amazing."

But nothing ever lasts, some dudes lost 45 grand of LA's money. Rich tried to calm him down, but LA went off. It could have been a war, but cooler heads prevailed. Sides were chosen and dudes squared off. LA and Rick teamed up with Sean Mo, but a lot of people on the street thought Sean Mo was after LA's money. He allegedly had some goons run up into LA's mom's house. LA had a lot of people shooting at Sean Mo, like it was target practice after that. But that was life in the drug game.

"Rich and LA were getting away with it. I felt the opportunity was there." AZ said of his decision to join LA and Rich in the drug game. "I was messing with Rich's sister, Patricia Porter." AZ was holding guns and drugs for LA and Rich in the cleaners he worked at. He kept getting more and more involved.

"I started when I was 17-years-old." AZ said. When the movie Scarface came out, the story of Tony Montana and his lust for money and power inspired young kids in ghettos across the country. "Scarface was like a big commercial to sell drugs." AZ said. "I believed that movie put it in me that I could do it. The Dominicans opened up the market so anyone could come Uptown and get it."

That same year a Colombian cocaine supplier approached AZ about selling cocaine for him. "AZ brought something new to the game." Patricia Porter said. "He came out with some shit were he was selling the bottles for $10." Coke at $10 a gram was unheard of. With the Colombian connect AZ joined Rich and LA and they started getting so many sales they blew up even bigger than before.

"They had mad drug crews. You need a crew to run a block. They called them gates in New York. Rich and them ran the whole block. They controlled that shit." The Harlem gangster says. AZ was getting the coke for dirt cheap and making 50 grand a week easy. He shared the wealth with his two friends.

"Rich came through the block in a gold Mercedes Benz. A tall heavy set, brown skinned kid was driving Rich. Rich explained to us that his man was new to the game and didn't really know many people This was AZ." The Harlem gangster says.

"I was lucky," AZ said. "My connect, Lulu, had a direct line to Colombian cocaine kingpin Pablo Escobar. There were no middlemen involved. I was able to get the best product at the lowest prices. I paid so little per kilo that I didn't have to dilute the coke to make money.

"Before long, Richard and LA were riding in my car. They couldn't understand it. They wanted to know what I did to get paid so fast. I told them how I operated and got them a brick, a kilo of cocaine. They set up shop on 144th Street and Seventh Avenue. Soon money came in duffle bags. We lived large. Rich got a new Jeep Wagoner. LA got a new black Jeep Laredo and rode around Harlem bumping the song Look at California by Maze featuring Frankie Beverly." But the good times wouldn't last.

LA was shot in front of the Rooftop skating rink. The Rooftop was a popular roller skating rink and club on 155th Street and Eighth Avenue. Everybody in the hood went to the Rooftop. LA, who was a real good skater, spent a lot of time there. Rich had warned LA not to go there, because of the jealousy other dudes had in their hearts toward LA and Rich, but LA thought he was above the haters.

"LA was standing there telling Baby J and Jerome Harris his car was mean and Blood Clad came through and shot LA up. LA was like, 'Take me to the hospital,' but Baby J and Jerome let him die, because they didn't want to get blood in their car," the Harlem gangster says. "LA was finally taken to Harlem Hospital. "Tons of people went to the hospital to see if he was okay, but he died. It was a sad night for Harlem. A crowd of people stayed in front of the hospital all night, crying and hoping it didn't really happen. Everybody in the hood was a fan of LA's, whether they knew him or not. All of Harlem paid their respects."

Everything went wrong for Rich after LA's death. LA's murder devastated Rich, along with the whole 200 building at the Drew Hamilton projects. LA had taken care of a lot of people in the 144th and 143rd Street areas. "Rich was fucked up when LA got killed." The Uptown player says. "He didn't have no problem with nobody, niggas loved him. But that didn't stop him from getting murked." In the drug game, murder was instantaneous and could happen at any time. No one was above getting a bullet in the head.

"I never did know the story behind LA's death," AZ said. "But I remembered a prior incident in front of this Italian restaurant named 721. Rich, LA and Gee Moe waited for a dude to exit the restaurant, they confronted him. The next thing I knew, Rich and LA began to empty their guns out on the guy. The guy struggled to get up, then started returning fire. The guy wore a bulletproof vest that day and survived the shooting. I later found out this was Blood Clad."

Talk on the streets revealed that Blood Clad killed LA. LA had suspected he was involved in the robbery of his mother's house a month earlier. The streets knew Blood Clad killed LA in retaliation for his earlier shooting. Blood Clad lost his life in the streets years later, but he was always remembered as the one who killed LA. After LA's death, things got real hot. Detectives were all over the place. A lot of dudes blamed Rich for LA's death. They thought Rich was jealous of LA.

"That was because of Rich," The Harlem gangster says. "LA was with Doo Wop. They thought Doo Wop would go at Rich, but it never happened. Rich was scared, he didn't want to get at Doo Wop. They were young gangsters, Doo Wop had a team."

Even though his man was killed, Rich would go on to become one of the most respected and well-known individuals to come out of the 1980s crack era in Harlem. With LA gone Rich was all in and since AZ had the banging coke connect, Rich dived in headfirst.

Cocaine put Rich Porter on the map. It gave him wings and an ability to generate more money than he ever imagined. It seemed to the young hustlers in Harlem, that cocaine was the ticket out of poverty, and AZ with his Colombian hookup, was the man. He started supplying Rich and they put all their energy into hustling cocaine. It would become their life. And Rich Porter ran with it. Two things would come to define him- cocaine and Harlem.

"Alpo came later, after Rich got locked up. Alpo knew Rich. Rich was in a shootout with the kid that robbed LA's mother's house. Rich was his man. They say the same kid who robbed LA's house was the same kid who shot him. Rich was in a shootout with this kid and wound up getting busted in the shootout and was charged with attempted murder by the police. The other kid got away, but Rich got caught with a gun that had been fired. Rich copped out to the pistol charge and got six months." AZ said.

CHAPTER 2

UPTOWN

"New Rich Porter, the way I flip quarters."
Jay-Z, American Gangster

Back then the streets of Uptown, known as the Westside, were a stronghold for blacks and had been for decades. Due to his dark skin and swagger, Harlem natives thought Alpo was a local and were surprised to learn that he was from the Eastside, which was known as Spanish Harlem. Alpo would be with Tee Money, Joe Love, Ali Moe, Benny Hill, Black Monk, Thettles, Tone, Lil' Pop, Baby J, Lil' Black Butter, Shawn Barnes, Darryl Barnes, Eggy, Whitey, Gregarito and Bat Ross. He was hustling out of Amandale's Restaurant.

He was new to the Westside, but was making a name for himself. Alpo would come through 119th Street with his tiger striped pit bull, Rock. "Yo, what up with that nigga Rich?" Alpo asked. "I don't like none of them Uptown niggas, especially when they was coming down 119th Street. I wanted to say something then, but just left it alone." Alpo was always bold and jumping out there to get noticed. He liked to be the center of attention.

"LA got killed outside of the Rooftop around 1985," Alpo

said. "So me and Rich's relationship became real strong and we became the best of buddies. Rich and I used to like the same cars, we were the first young dudes to bust out with the convertible BMW's, then the new Jeep."

A part of getting drug money was about betting and gambling on everything. Alpo would make $100 bets that his pit bull Rock could leap over a car without touching it. Someone would always take the bet. "Up Rock, up Rock, over the car," Alpo said and Rock would jump over the car. Alpo always won the bet. Alpo couldn't stand to lose and was always talking business.

Not long after Rich got locked up, Alpo went to jail on some bullshit charge. He met Rich at Rikers Island or so street legend holds. They met each other and became acquaintances. But since LA got murdered when Rich was on lock, he needed a new partner to watch his back. He saw Alpo as that dude. They became tight and joined forces. Before Rich went to jail, he had heard all about Alpo. The kid from the Eastside was making noise in the streets. Rich knew the Alpo wasn't afraid to bust his guns and would be a good addition the team.

Once Alpo teamed up with Rich, dudes were saying that Alpo thought he was the new LA. "Rich always said I reminded him of LA," Alpo said. "I was filling that spot that LA left when he got killed." The two would go on to form a new dynamic duo for Harlem's streets. Rich Porter never lost a beat, he just re-upped and had Alpo at his side. A flashy up and coming gangsta riding shotgun.

"Stick ups was his intro to the ghetto superstar life, but going to Rikers was his intro to the big cash and plug that led him to what everyone already knows about." The East River boriqua says. Rich plugged Alpo into AZ and his cocaine waterfall. Alpo would never look back. He had finally realized his cocaine dreams.

"I heard AZ was a young cat getting it, so I stepped to him. He was like come see me. I heard about you." Alpo said. "I didn't see him after that. I was waiting for him to get back at me. It was alright, because I was still doing my thing. I was eating, so it was all good." Once a dealer got money, they got power and respect. In AZ's case, everyone wanted to join the team. Including Alpo.

"I was at a game on 139th Street," AZ said. "I had just got in my car and pulled off and this motorcycle was tailgating me and shit, so I pulled over in front of my store on 145th Street. Alpo got off the motorcycle and took off his helmet to shake my hand. He said, 'Yo, Rich and I was doing something and since Rich got locked up I ain't got nowhere to get nothing from.' I told him, 'I'll speak to Rich and if Rich says it's all good, we'll take care of business.'

"Alpo wanted to be that nigga so bad. He used to come around every day, 'Yo, what up, A? Wanna ride with me?' Or 'A, could I hold that car?' He was the type of person that would push his way into the house. I gave him something on consignment and he would pay me back. I put Alpo on. I bought him an Impulse from the Volvo dealership for 17 grand. I had 50 grand in the trunk of my car so it was nothing. After that it seemed like he would do anything I'd tell him to do. I blessed Alpo when I met him. He always paid me on time." With the introduction through Rich Porter to AZ, Alpo came up.

"AZ bought me my first car, a black Impulse." Alpo said. "I wasn't really getting paid, but he was looking out. He felt he owed me this car because I was so loyal to him. I was his lieutenant at this time. I was taking care of business. He paid $17,000 for the car. Put a system in it and some BBS's on it. I got it for bottling up, hanging people out windows, shooting and all that.

"The night I stepped to him he had a couple of workers around. Some kids tried to shoot him, stick him up or something. He was telling me and as he was he was getting more frustrated. I was like, 'What are you gonna do?' He wanted to find them. I was like bet. I just needed 15 minutes. I had to go to the Eastside and get my guns.

"So while I did this, his workers go get whatever they had.

When I get back there's only one guy there. I notice AZ didn't say anything. I came back with two guns. We ended up finding one of the kids and busted him up. He got away and ran in his building; we were trying to kill this kid.

"To make a long story short I ended up beating the kid. I was trying to throw him out the second floor window. I was doing this because he robbed my man. I wanted to let him know he couldn't do this. I tried to throw him out the window, but I didn't succeed. I tried to tie his neck up and throw him out the window just to let him hang." Alpo was well versed as a gun thug and he had a violent streak.

"Alpo was from the Eastside, or Spanish Harlem, half black, half Puerto Rican, pretty boy thug." AZ said. "Rich gave me the green light to work with Po and I gave him some work and shared my recipe for making money. He never looked back. Once he made up his mind to do something, Po made it happen. He was assertive like that." Alpo was used to seizing opportunities which presented themselves.

"I ended up asking AZ if he could give me some bottles, this was the powder thing." Alpo said. "I told him I was going to take them on the Eastside. He was reluctant at first, but he told me to get back with him. I ended up getting back to him and one thing led to another and I got the bottles from him. I was doing my thing on the Eastside, flipping the bottles. I kept coming back to AZ. He was like, 'Damn, you flipping those like that.'

"I wasn't really flipping them. I was taking money out of my stash and paying him. I wanted him to believe I was flipping it like that. I stepped to him again, this time about going half and half on a store on the Eastside. He said alright and I got the store for 10 grand. I had the store for a little while, but the money wasn't coming in fast enough for me. So I asked AZ to put me down with him. I wanted to be a part of his crew.

"After that day, I was running with AZ. Now I'm down with him. I'm one of his soldiers. AZ is who I need to work with; he's the one I need to impress. I had no problem with the grind. I started from the bottom. I went with AZ and never looked back. So I'm down with AZ, doing all his dirty work." Some Uptown dudes acted like AZ unleashed Alpo on the Westside and criticized him for it. They couldn't deal with Alpo's gangster.

"Partly from jealousy, cats on the street told me I created a monster," AZ said. "They wasted no time reminding me of Alpo's humble beginnings or his reputation as a stick up kid. I wasn't the type that liked to gossip. I was chasing paper. I never took the bad words about Alpo seriously. I never liked when a cat would shit on the next man to gain respect. I didn't get down like that.

"I didn't care about Alpo's background and I didn't see him as a threat. He never did anything to violate me. He always paid on time and he played fair. I was the one who set him up in the game. Alpo and I became tight. I honestly felt I could trust him with my life. He was loyal to me." But a snake like Alpo was only loyal to the dollar and in truth, he was a force of nature unleashed on Harlem. A chaotic force that left destruction in his path.

"When Alpo was messing with my man JJ from 2250 he had a dust spot on 116th. He started coming Uptown with AZ and Kato and the kid, Travis, from Grant projects." The Harlem gangster says. "Vito from 117th and Manhattan bought Alpo a Honda Accord with the pop up lights. He had my sister in his car. I told him don't fuck with my sister. He said, alright Babyface and left her alone."

AZ was already established; he had a game room called the Jukebox on 145th Street between Seventh and Eighth Avenue. "My brother Kev, my man Stan, Lou and a bunch of other cats had the joint jumping. Chico and my man Dog Food provided security, we had a jukebox that played actual music videos, a variety of arcade games and shakes, it was off the hook. We blasted the hottest rap songs out- Larry's Dance Theme by Grand Master Flash, King of Rock by Run DMC and The Freaks Come Out at Night by Whodini. My spot became a favorite hangout in the hood and my whole crew was getting paid." AZ said.

The Jukebox was getting popular and all the stick up kids

started coming out of the woodwork, trying to get paid. They robbed the spot, trying g AZ's gangster but he wasn't with that part of the game, he tried to play fair. Plus he had so much money. "I stepped to AZ I was like, 'We got to put the murder game down.'" Alpo said, convincing AZ. "We found out who was setting it up and snatched him. Threw him in a van and made them tell us who the rest of them were. I was in charge of that situation. The bodies were found on 145th and Eighth Avenue. The stick up thing stopped after that of course. That's when AZ felt it just wasn't worth it to him."

AZ was rocking shit out of his store, but it started getting hot. "One time the police rolled in there," AZ said. "It was me, Alpo, Kato, Stanley, Lou, Whip, the whole click. Nobody had no drugs on them. The spot was too hot so I said, 'Fuck this, who wants this spot?' Alpo took it. He started making money, buying cars, big ass jewelry. He bought a ring that said Alpo all in diamonds, he would buy a motorcycle, crash or dent it, get off the bike and just give that shit to anybody there. He wanted to be that nigga." With the Jukebox, Alpo inherited a gold mine.

"That was the day I started doing my thing," Alpo said. "I knew what I had to do. I'd been down for a while. AZ was getting the coke and giving me enough for my spot. I knew I had a gold mine. I was willing to protect it by all means necessary. If that meant taking someone's life so be it. I had to put my own crew together. I met this kid Jay through my man Kato. Kato was strong and well respected. I explained the situation about the Jukebox to Jay. I put him down and let him know whoever else he put down was on him. I was only dealing with him. AZ was giving me the coke.

"He's hitting me. I'm hitting Jay. It's my spot. I'm paying for the bottles, for every loss and the work." Alpo blew up off the Jukebox. He came up in like six months. "Alpo was making money with AZ and talking about going out of town." The East River boriqua says. "He started making money and I'm going to say good cash, around 86-87." AZ was balling, Alpo was on boss status and Rich, the star of Harlem was on his way home, finishing up his time. The stage was set and this trio was getting ready to make history.

The H in Harlem was synonymous with hustler. A long lineage of hustlers had called the black Mecca home. In the 1970s, when heroin was the drug of choice, Frank Matthews, Nicky Barnes, Guy Fisher, Pee Wee Kirkland, Frank Lucas and Freddie Meyers all ruled the street of Harlem. They created a scene in the city that the young hustlers were becoming a part of.

During the late 1960s and early 70s, the drug addiction rate in Harlem was ten times higher than the New York City average and twelve times higher than the United States as a whole. Of the 30,000 drug addicts estimated to live in New York City at the time, more than half of them lived in Harlem. Property crime was rampant and the murder rate was six times higher than New York's average. By the 70s, the neighborhood no longer had a functioning economy and the economic life depended on the cash flow from illegal ventures. The kids who would come of use in the crack and hip-hop era were born during this downturn in Harlem's fortunes. Half of the children grew up with one parent or none. This proved monumental when the teenage drug lords hit the scene.

In the 1980s, there was a new drug of choice, called crack, and with crack came a new generation of hustlers. But on the crack filled streets of mid-80s Harlem, only three names mattered-Rich Porter, AZ and Alpo. Their combined brains, street smarts and ambition made them players in the New York drug trade by the time they were teenagers. Their story followed the rise and tragic fall of three lives linked by friendship, drugs, money and betrayal. They took Harlem by storm and controlled Harlem's drug trade, living by the code of the streets and pursuing the American Dream in the Mecca for blacks in New York City.

There was a great artistic legacy that came out of Harlem and it imprinted itself on the young hustlers, like a kind of cultural DNA. It was a Harlem thing, that hustler mentality, and in the hood it was all about how much a person could amass. During this time, hip-hop was a growing genre and culture. The young teenagers became fascinated with the music and immersed themselves in it. They would hang out in well-known Harlem nightspots like the Rooftop Skating Rink, that doubled as a nightclub. Stunting and flossing became the routine. Many young men were getting into the crack game and earning excessive amounts of money in return. For any young gun thugs, the drug game was the road to riches and fame. And Harlem was the place to be.

"We are just fly dudes," Sean P. Diddy said. "We just all around fly dudes and chicks. It's like we had swag before everyone else started saying it. That was the way we described ourselves. We are just known for being fresh. We are not dusty, bummy, crab ass dudes. Harlem has changed a little bit and there's been some transplants that have snuck their way in, but when you meet a real dude from Harlem and he says, 'What's up, B?' and he has his shit right, he got money in his pocket, he's fresh, his energy is right. That's Harlem. We're just fresh to death."

The way that the leaders of urban style and attitude move and express themselves in entertainment and the rap game nowadays has been entirely influenced by the cars and clothes, the style and swagger, and the walk and talk of the men and women from Harlem. It was a unique Harlem sophistication, a pizzazz or panache, that couldn't be found anywhere else in the world. And Alpo and Rich Porter were just following in the footsteps of the ghetto fabulous drug lords from the 1970s, except they didn't get rich off heroin, they got rich off crack.

Freebasing had a new label in 1985- crack cocaine. Heroin became second choice among drug users and crack houses took the place of shooting galleries. Young crack dealers emerged onto the streets and changed the drug world in Harlem into chaos. These young gun thugs became synonymous with the media's portrayal of the intimidating and menacing young black male. As the murder rates, drug addiction and overall violence of the time spiraled, the media created a publicity frenzy.

For those in Uptown, Harlem was split into two periods:

Before Crack and After Crack. "There was a profound change when that drug hit Harlem." The Harlem player says. "Heroin was a lifer drug, but people could function on heroin somewhat. Crack made people crazy. It created chaos. By some measures, the 1970s were the worst period in Harlem's history, but then crack hit."

Crack became so widespread because it didn't involve needles. People were scared of needles, with crack being meant to be smoked it took the fear out of it. And with the drug providing an immediate high, crack became very popular indeed. Crackheads would go behind the staircase in the tenement and smoke it. Crack became the first out drug. Guys would be on the street selling it while standing in doorways. They didn't give a fuck. In comparison, dealers back in the day would never think of selling drugs in the open. With everything out in the open, crack became the fastest way to the road of riches for those in the inner-cities.

"When crack came everybody got rich, the Colombians gave the Dominicans on the hill the coke and they gave it to all the hustlers on consignment. There were mad crack spots in Harlem," the Harlem gangster says. "There were all these base houses up and down 145th Street from Bradhurst Avenue all the way over to Broadway and Riverside at first and slowly they changed to crack."

Crack was popular with hustlers and customers because dealers could sell crack extremely cheap and make crazy profits. Crackheads loved the drug for its intense high and its cheap price at $10 a rock. The drug created such hysteria that long single file lines of people would stretch down an entire block as countless people waited to purchase crack. These drug cheese lines formed constantly all over Harlem, day and night.

Crack became the economy in the hood and the young crack dealers became under lords of the streets. Young princes of the ghetto with an endless cash flow, supersonic flash, new found materialism and hip-hop swagger. They were like the celebrities of the ghetto. Live and accounted for. The crack culture they perpetrated gave way to hip-hop and the drug lords were the first supporters of the rap movement.

But rap recording artists, in the mid-80s, hardly got noticed in Harlem. There were too many kingpins running around getting real money, not royalty money. Still, the rappers were on the scene and in the midst of the dealers. Harlem popped twenty-four seven and every event was turned into a fashion show. Anybody who was somebody in Harlem always passed through 112th Street. It represented the high court and forum where the epitome of ghetto coolness and style gathered and was expressed in full vitality. Everybody who was anybody rode through 112th Street.

Every young hustler made sure to ride in or around 112th Street on their way to gangster greatness. It was the strip to galavant though. The big boys and players would walk down the street through a parade of pitchers and fiends. "New York City was wild back in those days," the Spanish Harlem hustler says. "We had a lot of dudes come up out of here."

Harlem was all about style and the way you presented it to the neighborhood. All the kids would hang out and dudes would be pumping crack on the block. The game was wide open. Even the new rap superstars like LL Cool J were caught up in the scene. "I was spending like crazy." He said. "I bought a red Audi 5000. That was one of my favorite cars. In fact, I coined the phrase Audio 5000, which means I'm out. I had the biggest gold chains a neck could hold. I bought a mink coat.

"I would drive around Manhattan in a limousine with my boys drinking Moet and Cristal. And the women. There was even a time when I thought seriously about getting involved in the drug game. All the dealers around the way had status. They represented everything poor people didn't have and wanted so much: money, clothes, cars, property. They were living the African American dream, workin' the BMW, the black man's wish."

The renowned Harlem drug dealer had that smooth gangster etiquette and pedigree. He was well versed in the intricacies of the street and narcotics game. He made sure everything about himself was exclusive and first class. With cell phones the size of bricks, he was styling and profiling, living large and in charge.

In the crack era, only doctors and drug dealers carried beepers; and the drug lords had the 1-800 joints, they were doing it big in Harlem. One hundred forty fifth and 8th Avenue would turn into a car show. In the downtown sections of Harlem, it was all about who was getting the most money. Dudes flaunted their wealth in a variety of ways. To each individual, first class meant something different. But it all involved stunting to some degree.

Riding in OJ cabs was a status symbol. An OJ cab was one of the newest and trendiest car models that came out that year. "You only rode in an OJ cab if you were getting a lot of drug money." The Spanish Harlem hustler says. "If you were seen in an OJ cab, you were classified as a baller and all the females and gangsters admired you. They had all the latest hip-hop tapes and a booming sound system. You paid $50 an hour to ride around in one, smoking buds."

Frankie Beverly's Can't Let You Go was the drug dealer's anthem. All you heard was that and Heartbeat by Tanya Gardner blasting out of the OJ cabs. The cabs were like a party on wheels and a lot of the young drug lords ran their businesses out of them. They were drug entrepreneurs with major product and they were more than willing to travel to get paid. But they always stayed close to home. Shining in Uptown was their favorite past time and Harlem World was the place to be.

Harlem World was located at 116th Street and Lenox Avenue. Many fights and shootings took place at Harlem World. It was always Brooklyn against Harlem. The rappers and MC's would be at Harlem World battling. Kool Moe Dee and the Chief Rocker Busy Bee would be going at it on stage. Everything that was going down in the city, was going down in Harlem.

Club S&S was the hot spot too, it was above the famous Willies Burgers, where everyone hung out at. Club S&S and The

Zodiac Club were gambling dens where all the big hustlers congregated at and played C-low. Games of chance were big with the drug lords. They craved that opportunity to gamble away their fortunes with their illicit wealth. Either get rich or die trying.

The Rooftop, The Romper Room- big ballers would be in all the hot spots smoking coolies, otherwise known as crack weed. "Drugs are prevalent in entertainment." LL Cool J said. "It seems to go with the lifestyle- the money, the fast cars, jewelry, and the women. There are even some who feel they can't perform without some weed or a hit of cocaine. We would sometimes spice up the blunts with coke or angel dust. I would smoke just about anything."

When crack became king, it created a lawless and moral less world, but crack was also a hip-hop drug. People who weren't even getting high off crack felt the cultural effect it brought. The drug changed hip-hop. It influenced it and altered its growth. Crack and rap were born at the same time and grew of age together. Brothers to the same culture.

The crack dealer made hip-hop corporate, because the guys who emulated the crack dealers became rap stars. They wanted to be rough and ready and floss like the dudes on the block. "One hundred forty fourth Street was the block where all the girls passed through." The Uptown player says. "I honestly believed they just wanted to see Rich and Alpo." The lords of the ghetto were superstars, they encompassed all that was iconic in their era.

Since joining up with Rich and AZ, Alpo had developed a reputation as a serious force to be reckoned with. An enforcer with enough money and power, to terminate the lives and careers of any who opposed the trio. Alpo was a gorilla hustler. A man who made money where and how he wanted. No one stood in his way unless they were willing to die, not just kill, to make their point. That sort of bravery was uncommon even among gangsters.

The three amigos brought different personas to the game.

Rich was known for showboating, AZ was considered cool and calculating and Alpo was known to be reckless and trigger happy. "Alpo was a wolf, he took charge. Didn't nobody have to tell him how to move." The Uptown player says. "When he was working with AZ it was smooth. Rich ain't soft either. Both of these young niggas was going hard. Three the hard way, the mayors of Harlem. The youngest niggas to ever do it." They were kings of the Uptown court, gangster royalty.

"Rich and AZ, and then Alpo got into the fold, they used to be in front of Willies Burgers, 116th and Lenox Avenue. That used to be Harlem World," the Uptown player says. With the game and the hood on lock Alpo, Rich and AZ were in pocket. They did what they wanted, when they wanted. They were like movie stars in a feature film.

"All three of us were doing our thing," Alpo said. They were networking and making connections. The trio had many dealings with Mafioso Ian "En" Saporita before he was shot and killed in front of a bodega in Harlem. They hung out and partied with raps tars.

"I used to roll with a guy from Uptown," LL Cool J said. "He had the jewelry and the cars and the women and I wanted to be down. I would hang around him and he would let me weigh his stuff. At the time all I could think was, wow, he's doing his thing. But drug dealing is negative and destructive. At the same time it fulfills people's dreams and it's very attractive to a lot of poor black and Latino kids.

"All they see is the jewelry, the cars, the women, the good times. They see the results, but they don't see the paranoia, the spiritual death, the violence, the betrayal and the danger that goes hand and had with drug dealing. All the ones I've ever known wish they didn't have to do it. But back then, I was blinded by the so-called wealth." Because in Harlem, getting money was where it was at.

"If you couldn't get money in Harlem, you can't get no money," the Uptown player says. "If you getting money and you ain't got no crew, you gonna get bodied. Everybody carries guns in

Uptown. If you hustle in the city and don't carry a gun, you're crazy. The police didn't give a fuck back then. Alpo had his own people, Rich had his own people and AZ had his own people."

AZ was making a 100 grand a week selling cocaine. By 19, AZ was a cocaine wholesaler in Harlem. "AZ had that fish scale, that beige shit," the Uptown player says. "AZ had a connect in Windsor Terrace. Rich was fucking with Fritz. They would feed Alpo. When you got a connect like that, you can't do anything but blow up. He's trying to beat everybody's prices. These niggas getting real money."

Fritz was known as the consignment king in Harlem and on the wholesale tip he was the only one who could fuck with AZ, but Fritz only fucked with Rich. "Fritz didn't know Alpo and wasn't trying to know him. Alpo was flamboyant and Fritz didn't like that." The Uptown player says. "Fritz was on a whole other level, he was older than we were. He helped to make a lot of hustlers' realities come true."

AZ had an apartment on 133rd and Lenox Avenue at Lenox Terrace. He lived on the 9th floor and had a half court basketball spot in his apartment. That was the crew's hangout and headquarters. He kept things low profile, in comparison to Rich and Alpo. He figured he was in it to win it, playing the long game.

"The drug game was as simple as this; nobody could mess with me at the time. I had the best prices, the best connect and I was playing fair. Everybody was eating and all of Harlem was lit up." AZ said. "Getting money was simple, get the work, sell it and pay the connect."

At the Jukebox, between 7th and 8th Avenue, Alpo was killing them. "This was AZ's spot. Alpo had it with Big J. He started getting money around our way. Alpo had a serious gun game, but he was so grimy. Alpo was fronting with Big J's Saab for a week. Everybody thought it was Alpo's. He was a dirty dude like that. Big J was the dude that was keeping him up and that's how Alpo did him." The Harlem gangster says.

"Guy Fisher's daughter Ronda was talking to Big J and Alpo

tried to get at her. Big J was supposed to be his man. Big J bought Ronda a long coat at Roof of the Worlds, cost like $700. Alpo got jealous, slammed the girl's coat on the sidewalk. He was like that. Alpo had a pit bull named Crusher that used to be Uptown with Big J. Alpo had done some shit in Big J's car and he got shot up. He lied to Big J about his car. He was always lying to Big J, but Big J kept fucking with Alpo." Alpo had that affect on people; he was a charmer until the end. He was building a reputation in Harlem that was equal to Rich Porter's and LA's.

"The spot on 145th was moving eight bricks a day." Alpo said. "It was ridiculous. We had to tell people they had to line up on the other side of the street. At the time crack was beginning to blow up. I was able to flood it and give up good prices. If someone was selling for $20 I could sell the same size for $10.

"I was getting money and my name was blowing more and more. I was the kid from the Eastside that came to the Westside and was hitting all the women. They were calling me wild and crazy. I was just having fun. I was young. I was making such a name for myself in the crack game. AZ played fair. AZ was a good guy. We started getting real popular, we were getting it.

"I'm getting three to eight bricks from the connect and we're flooding 145th Street. I'm paying $14,000 and charging Big J 30 g's. The reputation was great at the Jukebox. People started putting crack spots around there. Big J started getting conniving. I was losing money. A little gunplay broke out. People were getting jealous. I left 145th Street and that's when my relationship with Rich started.

"Rich was just coming home from prison. I was already on 145th Street, so I was already established. If you knew LA, you know I was filling that spot he left. Rich, AZ and I were all doing our own thing. Rich and I used to have a lot of the same cars. We were the first young kids to bust out with the 7 series BMWs. I paid cash. The joints were hot and we were the first young guys out there with them."

Alpo had a stash house at 115th Street, between Manhattan and Morningside Avenues, it was a famous freebase house called Nitro's. In Alpo's freebase days, he owed a lot of vicious dudes money, but he never paid. He dared them to step to him and they didn't. He was getting a fearsome rep. Nobody wanted to fuck with him. If somebody even thought about doing something to Rich or AZ, Alpo would body them.

"Alpo was that person that had to be seen." The Spanish Harlem hustler says. "Po was like a daredevil, the Evel Knievel of the hood. He made it fun to get money. Alpo would follow cabs popping wheelies, yelling to people. Alpo would bet dudes about doing wheelies.

"'Bet I can beat you all going downtown doing a wheelie from 125th Street and Morningside to 116th and Morningside.' He would win the bets too. There were police car chases in Porches. Police chasing them. Alpo could drive. I've never seen a nigga drive like that in my life."

The dudes in Harlem were still learning about Alpo. He would get out of a cab laughing and the cab driver would say something to him in Spanish and Alpo would start talking back to the cabbie in Spanish. Dudes in Uptown bugged out on that. They didn't have a clue that Alpo was Spanish. Alpo didn't give a fuck about nothing either.

"Alpo disrespected those that didn't have respect for themselves." AZ said. "If you see somebody that's wild and crazy like that, with no respect for himself, how is he going to have respect for you." Alpo wasn't crazy around everyone though, he had his picks. He knew who to give respect to.

"Alpo was scared of Doo Wop, a dude who had big respect in Uptown," the Harlem gangster says. "Doo Wop wouldn't put Alpo on. Alpo had the Louis Vuitton coat and Doo Wop was riding up and down the street in a Porsche. Alpo had a lot of respect for Doo Wop, said he was a gangster, getting a lot of money." All the Harlem hustlers were scared of Doo Wop.

"One time, Kevin Chiles was throwing a bus ride party to Bear Mountain. We all went to Bear Mountain- me, Slugger, Eddie Lee, Doo Wop. They had a basketball game for 15 or 20 grand. Alpo could play ball, he was like that, he could have played college ball. Before the game Alpo came to Doo Wop and asked permission to act crazy and Doo Wop said, 'Knock your self out.' Doo Wop put half the money up for the basketball game and Alpo and them won, so Doo Wop told Alpo's team to come and get the money Uptown. But they never came, they were scared.

"Alpo always wanted to be the center of attention. Black Just from the Supreme Team was there and he wanted to take photos with Doo Wop and Alpo, but Doo Wop didn't want to take photos with Alpo." Alpo wasn't sensitive though, he just rolled with it. But he was real impulsive, he did tons of shit on the spur of the moment, just making it up as he went along. He thrived on shit like that.

"I recall riding up 128th near 8th Avenue." AZ said. "An older brother drove past us in a Corvette Sting Ray. It was one of the prettiest cars. Po honked the horn for the dude to pull over and he did. The guy pulled over and Alpo stepped to him. Within ten minutes Po made a deal he couldn't refuse, he wanted the guys car so bad that he offered to pay him a huge lump sum right on the spot. The guy agreed, so Alpo went to the trunk, pulled out a bag of money and handed it to the guy. Po pulled off in the Corvette."

Alpo could afford to do stuff like that because him and his crew were getting it. Teaming up with Rich Porter and AZ was the best move Alpo ever made. "They was hitting half of Harlem. Rich and Alpo was getting it." The Uptown player says, and their success inspired a huge following. They became the darlings of the drug world. Hip-hop hustlers extraordinaire, kings of Uptown.

CHAPTER 3

TRENDSETTERS

"I don't want to be like Mike/more like Po and Porter/getting shipments at the border." Shyne

"Alpo and Rich were ahead of their time," AZ said. "I often tell people that Rich, Alpo and I were popular like the Jackson's during the 80s and 90s. We were like ghetto celebrities. Some idolized us, others were jealous and some imitated us. People we didn't even know would come up running, trying to walk and talk with us. Some asked for autographs and others wanted to take pictures with us.

"Rich had a 16 valve Mercedes Benz, gold with gold piping, we was cruising and it seemed like everyday in front of the S&S club, like over a hundred people, just seemed to stop and look at us. Me and Rich were looking at each other, and Rich put the car in first gear and we started moving away real slow, Rich was like, 'Yo, muthafuckas looking at us like we stars or something,' and that's when I first realized that people was looking at us like AZ, Alpo and Rich."

A lot of the new jacks, dudes who were new to the game or fronting, were in the trio's faces. "Those niggas was setting trends and they weren't nothing but 16 years old." The Uptown player says. "Rich was the first nigga with a BMW when he was 16. They changed cars like niggas changed shoes. They had money like toilet paper, throwing 1000s in the air. Letting niggas get it. "Harlem niggas was the flyest around and in the city; they started that leaning all the way back in the car shit. Rich and Alpo were two of the flyest niggas in Harlem, they were like Batman and Robin, they had the jewels that matched their cars." The trio lived like kings, flashing expensive jewelry and driving luxurious cars throughout the streets of Harlem.

"Usually I tried to make my jewelry match the car I wanted to drive at the time," AZ said. "When I bought my BMW 735 I sported a gold number 7 flooded with diamonds. It cost me about 12 grand. When I bought my first Benz I wore a Benz car medallion that had more ice than a freezer. I had another medallion featuring a top hat, white gloves and a cane to represent a gentleman. Most medallions I owned cost between 10 g's and 20 g's, but we bought them like socks back then, at my highest peak I was making a hundred thousand a week. I was 19 years old."

Young kids in Uptown embraced Alpo, Rich and AZ's trends and rocked gold chains, sported foreign cars and had thousands of dollars in their pants for pocket change. "There's a lot of similarities between the drug game and rap game," LL Cool J said. "In both cases young people are looking for power and a voice in a powerless situation. The life of a rap artist coming up at first is similar to that of a dealer or even a wise guy, a Mafioso. You got the knot of cash in your pocket, the cars, the money, the jewelry, the walk."

The Harlemnites were young blacks who were on hustler status, but they were drug dealers who ran their organizations like companies. They had the big cell phones before anyone else. They had the big 18 carat gold medallion, with diamonds and rubies, and the matching diamond ring and bracelet. All the young go-getters were wearing jewelry like that on every block.

"When I started making some money in the rap game it was

some of the big time dealers from around my way who put me down with the best known jeweler in the city- Manny's, in Manhattan's diamond district, the real deal." LL Cool J said. "It was nothing for me to drop $20,000 on a chain or a ring, just like the big time dealers. Before then, I bought my gold on Jamaica Avenue."

Harlem started the bling-bling fashion. Big rope chains weren't even popular back then, it was all about name chains, big 10 carat Chinese letter name chains. Alpo, Rich and AZ started with all the bling and their names started ringing bells throughout the city. They were the first crew to use beepers to communicate. The trio was flamboyant and ruthless.

"A lot of dudes in my city, New York, ain't ready for that gunplay," the Spanish Harlem hustler says. "That dude Alpo put in work and I can't think of anyone besides Boy George and Spanish Chicki from Hunts Point in the Bronx that wasn't influenced by him, even if they were out before him. Queens and Brooklyn dudes excluded." Alpo wasn't afraid to put in work, but Rich was that super fly, popular type of guy. Alpo was feared, but Rich was loved.

"Rich was revered while Alpo was de-tested," Velma Porter, Rich's mother said. But in the drug game it's better to be feared than loved. Everyone knows that. Respect is earned looking down the barrel of a gun. And Alpo was that serious gun thug. On the street it was like, "Yo, that's Alpo. Nigga on top of the world, son." Dudes were all up on Alpo's jock trying to be associated and affiliated with him.

"He had so much fun. He made young cats wanna get money, he was like a superhero to niggas in the hood. Money was nothing to him. He had that charismatic shit about him." The Spanish Harlem gangster says. "Alpo was crazy for real, but he was funny at the same time." Alpo was about that gunplay, but he was also about that swag. Plus he would cross a motherfucker in a minute. That was just the nature of the drug game. But in Harlem Alpo set the scene.

"Niggas was buying minks, jewelry, BMWs, Saabs with the

interior." The Uptown player says. "When Alpo got that money he let muthafuckas know by creating his own style, he bought his shit from Dapper Dans, he blew that shit up." Dapper Dans was a popular tailor shop in Harlem, on 125th Street and Madison Avenue.

"Dan made his living by purchasing authentic fabrics from top designers like Gucci, MCM and Louis Vuitton and creating custom made coats, jackets, baseball caps, pants and suits that the original designer didn't even make. If you bought something from Dan, you knew it was one of a kind." AZ said. Dapper Dan would make a Gucci or Louis Vuitton jacket or suit, and the hustlers in Harlem like Alpo, would rock it like they were movie stars.

"Alpo just took that shit to the next level when the serious cash came in," the East River boriqua says. "Dapper Dans, laced with whatever he could. Alpo was a flashy dude always so he just turned it up when he had more money to spend on clothes. That nigga was setting the fashion trends that muthafuckas wish they could keep up with. The dude was like that back then."

Timberland boots were also an Uptown thing. In the hood, it was all about styling and profiling, going to the Rucker and seeing the ghetto superstars up close and personal. With the late model European whips, the truck jewelry and the wads of cash, they carried around as pocket change, the Harlem drug lords knew they were the shit.

The 80s belonged to Alpo, Rich and AZ. When the guns started going off, Alpo would even sport a Gucci bulletproof vest. He was always on the cutting edge, clothing wise. They also shopped at A.J. Lester's on 125th Street. For Harlem, A.J.'s was the spot. They'd go to Phil Cromfields in Times Square on 49th Street and Broadway, dropping tens of thousands at a time. Spending money, fronting, stunting and having fun. That's what it was all about.

"Alpo was fun, but it depends on your idea of fun," the Spanish Harlem hustler says. "We went to see Eddie Murphy's Coming to America at Loew's on 86th Street, and Alpo had to get up and go to the bathroom and like seven dudes got up and escorted him, and instead of coming back Alpo lit an M-80 and threw it in the crowd and dudes started shooting and we all ran.

"Needless to say, we all met on 89th Street and 2nd, at a spot called Midnight Express, a Greek diner and someone told us a little girl got shot, that her knee was injured and Alpo pulled out a knot and said, 'Here's $10,000, tell the bitch to buy a new knee.'" For real Alpo didn't give a fuck. He craved chaos and controversy.

"He was by Willies Burger, he was with Niece," The Harlem gangster says. "He was driving a white M3 with an eight ball on top of the gear shift, black pipes all around. It was mean. He had a BMW chain, plus a bracelet and ring, along with the white on white M3. The small M3. Rich had an ice blue one.

"Alpo is giving money away. Niece wants to go, so she starts complaining. Alpo pulled Niece to the side and kicked her in the stomach, he got her pregnant and told her to get an abortion, she didn't so he said he'll give her one with the kick." Alpo could be vicious to anyone at any time. It didn't matter. It was like he would flip a switch. He was fun, but he had a twisted sense of humor.

"Alpo threw $1000's off the roof of Wilson projects and muthafuckas went berserk trying to scoop up as much of the singles as possible," the Spanish Harlem hustler says. Being unpredictable was part of his personality and MO. To the streets Alpo was chaos incarnate. He loved to create drama and be in the mix.

"We were at this kid's birthday party, it was Darryl Barnes birthday. It was a minkathon." AZ said. "Alpo wore a full length Louis Vuitton goose down. The party was at the Celebrity Club on 125th Street, right next to Dapper Dan's clothing store. Darryl had on a sequin jacket, mink coat and all that. It was one of them Big Willie parties. Everybody was dressed in sequin jackets and mink coats. Everybody was dressed proper.

"It was time to blow the candles out and this nigga Alpo picks up the cake and smashes it in Darryl's face, that's just how he was. He had to have people looking at him. He told Darryl, 'Happy Birthday, nigga.' Alpo was smiling like he did something good, people was looking at him like, 'You idiot.' That shit never bothered Rich."

Cars, jewelry and nice houses were the key ingredients to flossing or showing off wealth. Hustlers also did this by maintaining a nice wardrobe. It was a matter of keeping up with the Jones. "Rich liked to handle his business. He was real neat, never wore the same outfit twice, kept a haircut, kept his jewelry sparkling, he would wear a ring with one stone worth 7 or 8 grand, a Rolex on his wrist. Carried himself real respectable. Not into all that crazy shit," AZ said.

"He was always sharp. Although he dressed casually, he always wore high quality, expensive clothes, he never came out looking sloppy. He was always extremely neat and clean. Alpo wore expensive jewelry too. Alpo had rings customized to fit over four fingers, he had one ring like this that spelled out his name in diamonds, it resembled a very fancy set of brass knuckles.

"Alpo was the first cat to rock the four finger ring. Today rappers flaunt extravagant jewelry covered with expensive diamonds, it's now very common in hip-hop culture, but I believe we started that trend in the early 80s." AZ said. To the rappers like LL Cool J, Rich and Alpo were the real celebrities. Rich and Alpo created images and personas that were emulated in the rap game. "You got all the rappers acting like they want to be drug dealers," the Harlem player says. "Alpo would pay the rappers $200 for a mixtape as long as they said his name on it. Alpo paid 15 grand for a big ring that said Alpo. Then LL Cool J and Biz Markie started wearing four finger rings too. I remember when hip-hop really started catching on. It was really influenced by these guys."

The stories that Biggie, Jay-Z and Easy E told, they all came from the streets. All of these guys came out of the crack culture that infected the streets in the 80s. It really had a big impact on hip-hop culture. All the rappers from New York wanted to be down with the scene that the drug dealers created. It was a case of jacking styles and copycatting.

"That was part of growing up." LL Cool J said. "Early on in my career I used to hang with my friend Big Chuck. We used to be Uptown all the time, we used to hang out with Alpo, Rich Porter and AZ. Those are the guys that taught me the lifestyle. Those are the guys that raised me in a lot of ways. Even though I was releasing music, I was still a teenager and they were a little bit older. Those were the cats that taught me little things.

"I would do shows in Virginia and they would come down with all the cars, come backstage and drive right in. I was as impressed as anybody else was. I was just happy to be hanging out and learning so much. The things I was bringing to the world like the big LL Cool J rings and the ice and the diamonds, the champagne and panthers and all that stuff, that's stuff I was living because of them.

"I had got that from them when we was all vibing together. And the world wasn't even ready for it. People were booing me for the things they celebrate today. Leading up to Walking with the Panther in 1989 I was hanging out with them in Harlem. That album was heavily influenced by that, the jewelry, the champagne, the bottles, the Benz's and the furs and all that."

Alpo, Rich and AZ's flashy styles influenced rappers and street culture in general. The teenage drug lords were trendsetters of epic proportions. From crack cocaine kingpins to inner-city demigods, the trends they set still resonate today. With the Gucci leather suits, fur coats and chains, rappers from LL to Cam'ron have bit their style and made them iconic in hip-hop. From Harlem, their attitudes and style spread to the world. They influenced hip-hop clothing in the same way they influenced hip-hop car buying and jewelry. Harlem drug dealers exposed the rappers to clothing styles from stores like Dapper Dan and his Harlem customized shop. Through music videos and rap magazines these fashions have gone international.

LL would go to 145th and Amsterdam, the big drug spot and hangout. He would chill on the block, soaking in the atmosphere. LL got his whole swag from Alpo. Rakim was wearing the MCM, Louis Vuitton suits; they got all that from Alpo. The kid set a lot of trends. He was the real superstar. Along with Rich and AZ, they ran Harlem. They were the essence of what it was to be fly.

LL Cool J and Doug E. Fresh would run errands for Alpo and Rich. They used to clown Doug E. Fresh. They didn't even realize back then that he would blow up like he did and become a hip-hop pioneer. To the drug dealers these dudes were just little shorties on the block. The rappers were wannabe's to the drug dealers.

Biz Markie and MC Shan, they were around all the time, trying to bask in the limelight of the princes of Harlem, just like everybody else. Alpo would be on the block with the Levi suit, Black high top Reeboks and a Champions sweatshirt. He'd have an Israeli Uzi on a strap under his Levi suit jacket. Ready to get busy.

Alpo was around Puffy, before he was even Puff Daddy. Back when Puff was a dancer for Father MC. LL Cool J would buy coke from Alpo, right about the time that the Walking with the Panther album came out. Eric B and Rakim's Make 'Em Clap To This along with KRS-One and Kool G's raps made it cool to be a rap artist. When dealers like Alpo saw the rappers they would be like, "That's my nigga." Giving the rap dudes dap and props in the hood. They embraced the rappers and culture they spawned.

Over 20 years before "making if rain" became a catchphrase, AZ, Rich and Alpo were throwing $50's in the air everywhere they went. They had money to burn and they flaunted their wealth. The rap celebrities and dudes in the burgeoning hip-hop industry emulated their lifestyle and tried to be down.

"I remember when Rich gave Teddy Riley his money to get started. I remember when LL Cool J used to come through and rap on the corner just to stand next to us on 132nd." AZ said.

Alpo and Rich were the real stars back then and the rappers clung to them. Trying to move in the same circles and be a part of the scene. They wanted to be affiliated with the hustlers to get street cred.

"Alpo saved LL Cool J's life at the Rooftop nightclub one time and in return LL took Alpo on tour with him on his first tour to Hawaii." The Spanish Harlem hustler says. "One time Alpo punched LL in the face at the Apollo because all the girls were giving LL more attention. Alpo couldn't stand that. LL didn't do nothing. They were beefing, but not really. Alpo beat up Keith Sweat over a girl. He chased Keith Sweat through Grant projects, shooting at him for fucking with the same girl he did and Keith Sweat was butt-ass naked. Alpo started fucking Pepa from Salt-n-Pepa when the movie Delicious came out."

Alpo loved to be the center of attention and the subject of discussion. He practically lived at the Rooftop. The Rooftop attracted a young wild crowd that didn't give a fuck. This resulted in robberies, shootings and murders at the club. The club was off the hook and attracted all the main players from the black underworld.

"I never understood why Alpo wanted to chill in a club like that. Why go to a spot full of rival dealers who might be jealous of you? Why put yourself in the line of fire just to show off? Alpo went to the Rooftop to show off his cars, clothes, women and jewelry, it was a big competition. It's impossible to floss wealth without attracting envy. Jealousy is always a problem in the drug game. Hot cars and iced out jewelry drew attention." AZ said.

Alpo craved that attention. He wanted it. Customized cars, fine women, props and street respect were what he chased after. Those were the material things he wanted and why he went so hard to attain his cocaine dreams. He spent money like crazy to show that he was the man. It was all about the show to him. Alpo's and Rich's way of life would influence music, clothing and even Hollywood.

"Alpo was well known because he went everywhere, he wanted to be known. He wanted to be popular." The Spanish Harlem hustler says. "Alpo was a freak for that shit. 'Yo, let's go to Queens, let's go to Forty projects, let's go over to Baisley projects.' He'd say. Every 4th of July he'd set off a bunch of fireworks out the back of his Bronco, he'd spend 20 grand on the fireworks and light up the whole sky. He did some real John Gotti type shit.

"Alpo was buying everything, he didn't stash his money. He'd buy all the new whips before they even came out. The radio stations would give Alpo and Rich shout outs. They had the cars kitted out and the sound systems were blasting. They had all the hot whips and hot accessories, including the dime pieces on their arms. Alpo was buying girls new BMWs. Paying for trips, buying jewelry, diamonds, mink coats. The nigga would pull up in a different car every day. Were they all his, who knows, but I'm going to say that his money was big time long, because nobody is going to lend a nigga a Porsche or Benz or BMW to the local dude on the corner."

The young hustlers would go to the Rooftop, the hottest club in Harlem and The Fever. The Rooftop was off the hook and the S&S club was rocking. Different drug dudes would be there. They'd be sporting the four wheelers and black Kawasaki's, before the Ninjas came out. They were always competing with the cars. Like who had the flyest whip. Dudes were riding Jetta's at first, 190 Benz's, Saab's with BBS rims on them. They would all come through with their whips to Willies Burgers and front.

It wasn't just all about the cars though; dudes were showing their gangster in many ways. Alpo was a serious gun thug. He'd handle all the beefs for the trio. Alpo wanted to beat dudes up and shoot them. He wanted to be seen and get his respect. He wanted to be feared and admired. AZ thought Alpo was too loud and obnoxious, but others respected his gangster.

"Alpo brought adrenaline to the hood, he was standing up doing 20 block wheelies. Evel Knievel got nothing on Alpo. He would come on a motorcycle, stunting and fronting for the crowd that would be gathered to watch him on the block, or in front of Willies Burgers or the Rooftop. Doing wheelies and all that shit." The Spanish Harlem hustler says.

"He'd be riding motorcycles up and down 8th Avenue at two or three o'clock in the morning, breaking bottles, causing havoc. Him and Rich were like the main attraction. It was their styles, their voices, the way they talked that the streets loved. Black Just and Bimmy from the Supreme Team used to come up to Harlem all the time to hang out with Rich and Alpo." Alpo loved to be center stage and most times he was.

"Alpo became very annoying. He was out there broadcasting." AZ said. "That's how Alpo was. One time we was coming from a hotel with some girls and the Rooftop skating rink was on 155th Street and 8th Avenue and he was like, 'Yo, take me to the garage,' because he was in my car and he wanted to get his car to show it off. He had like 20 cars stashed in the parking lot.

"Alpo was coming up 7th Avenue, cops chasing him and crashed the BMW and left it, gave it away, told dudes, 'Get it fixed and you can have it.' That's the type of shit he would do. Alpo did a lot of wild shit, he used to go and buy cars for cash. He'd bring like six different girls. He was known for hitting other known niggas' bitches on tape and showing it on the wall at the club like a movie. "He had sex with a few girls and showed that shit back on videotape, but the girls was stupid enough to want to be in the movies. He used to put the tapes in the camcorder and bring it outside and blow chicks up. Niggas used to look in the monitor and see all kinds of chicks from the neighborhood; he would bring it to the Rooftop." Alpo was scandalous like that, he didn't give a fuck.

"Bouncy B, Doo Wop and other hustlers would be at the Rooftop. That was the main hangout. Alpo was the center of attention. Pretty boy Puerto Rican type nigga," the Spanish Harlem hustler says. "He would fuck all the hustlers girls, record it and show it on the VCR at the Rooftop, he would put shows on with the Ninja, pop a wheelie down the whole block, cops chasing him, can't catch him. He'd put on shows for 20 minutes with cops chasing him on the bike."

Alpo was a big gambler too. "They had pots of 50, 60 grand at the C-low games. Alpo would win and give that shit out." The Harlem player says. "Twenty thousand on the floor and a group of ten people standing around placing bets, gambling was part of the drug life and was responsible for the rise and fall of many drug empires. With Alpo, the money flowed and it's said he was the first black man in Harlem to own a Lamborghini."

Alpo and Rich were at the center of everything happening in Harlem. "We'd ride past the Rucker in the whip. Hanging on 137th. That's where we'd be at," AZ said. "S&S Club, where everyone hangs out. Pull up by Willies Burgers. The whole crowd was looking at us."

Alpo would be at the Rucker watching the games. In 1989, at the EEC Championship, a team of youngsters, called the Future Pros, was playing a more experienced older team called the Jays. Alpo was court side and had bet big money on the Jays, who were the favorites. It wasn't looking good for the Jays though and Alpo didn't want to lose his money.

Midway through the first half of a close game, Malik "The Freak" Sealey, who went on the play in the NBA, snatched a rebound and zipped it down the court to The Future himself, Malloy Nesmith, a Rucker Park magician, who dunked the ball hard. With an ecstatic crowd smelling a possible upset, a pair of large brown pit bulls along the Jays sideline began smelling the flesh of the two officials working the game.

Alpo was unhappy the way some of the calls had gone to that point in the contest. So he loosened up a bit on both leashes during a timeout and shouted toward both referees while the players from each team were huddled. "Yo refs, you muthafuckas make one more bad call and I'm gonna turn both your asses into dinner." As Alpo spoke he was walking toward the officials, his pit bulls growling and the crowd went silent.

Finally there was just the sight of Alpo's hungry dogs at mid court and the sound of their growls. The atmosphere had suddenly turned from festive to frightening. Frozen with fear, both refs began backpedaling. The whole crowd, even the players got real scared. Guys from both teams tried to calm Alpo down and convince him to get his dogs out of there.

When play resumed, the Future Pros continued to outclass the Jays and won. Alpo lost his money, but he made his point. That was just how he did it. He didn't give a fuck. He courted chaos and reveled in it. Whereas Alpo was crazy, Rich was smooth, a real debonair type of dude.

"The streets made and ordained him the prince of the streets. A Rich Porter only graces the pages of time once in a thousand years," Velma Porter said. Rich was the first to buy and sport the black BMW 528i. He made that shit cool, just like he made the Timberlands and clothes he wore cool. Rich, and other hustlers around the globe, were indirectly responsible for increased sales of BMWs, Saabs and Timberlands. They had a huge impact in what was hot in pop culture.

Rich's love of cars led to a large fleet of luxury vehicles, some of which he gave away. He kept a garage in Manhattan filled with dozens of high end cars. He collected exotic vehicles like kids were collecting Hot Wheels or Star Wars figures. He graduated to the big time early and spared no expense in buying what he wanted, when he wanted.

"Rich took care of a lot of niggas in New York." The Uptown player says. "Gave a lot of stuff out- turkeys, money, everybody on the whole block would get something." Rich Porter would splurge, but he would stack also. His hustle game was tight.

"Rich and I had the same ideology on the game," Kevin Chiles from Don Diva magazine said. "He and I often talked about different real estate ventures. Rich owned property in New York and Florida. He used to travel a lot, while most dudes never left the block."

Everybody always thought that AZ and Rich were tight, but Alpo shared a different opinion. "They had two different styles," Alpo said. "AZ thought Rich was too extravagant and Rich thought AZ was a punk. Rich also had a problem with AZ opening a spot right across from him on 132nd Street. Rich was selling crack and AZ was selling powder coke. Rich didn't appreciate that, but AZ had a daughter by Rich's sister Pat. Unless you knew them, you would have never known they were brother and sister. Like I said, I knew Rich and he cared about one person and that person was Rich."

Alpo was on one million and full blast crazy 24/7, but Rich was more quiet and laid back, even though he was styling. He liked hustling in Harlem and didn't want to go out of town to hustle when Alpo started urging him to. Rich got all the love in Harlem. He was happy there. He stayed in Harlem and got money. Alpo made some connections and started going out of town to get money. Alpo was generating a lot of heat in Harlem, so he started going to Washington, DC and selling keys for 24 grand a piece, almost doubling what he paid for them.

"Around this time guys were going to Myrtle Beach for the motorcycle weekend," Alpo said. "We all threw our bikes on the trailer and went. Rich and AZ didn't want to go. We all get to Myrtle Beach early the next morning, but I didn't see anything I liked. I am driving my new 7 series BMW. I was like I'm out of here; I'm going to Virginia Beach.

"It was Labor Day weekend. All the colleges were down there. It was off the hook. We rolled into town with the seven and those Five Star rims. Everybody was looking at us. There were girls everywhere. There were a bunch of DC kids down there who were getting it. They said if I ever came to DC to give them a call. They needed an outside connect. I'm starting to meet different dudes and they're telling me what the bricks are going for. I go back to New York and bought me a Chevy Blazer. This was the popular truck down there and I wanted to blend in.

"While I was in New York I met some other DC cats and we exchanged numbers. I met them in Dapper Dans. They told me about a Patti Labelle concert in DC. I asked AZ if I could hold his 190 with the Louis Vuitton seats. I went down there. Just me, the Louis Vuitton seats, and my big ass name ring. My Gucci and MCM jackets. DC was really into name brands. So when they saw me they went crazy. "Virginia Beach became my spot every year. One year I had LL Cool J and Eric B and Rakim rolling with me. I met some DC girls, Karen and Inga. Rich and I invited them to New York and decided to buy some Porsches to let the girls see how we were rolling. We told the dealer we had 75 grand in a paper bag for two 944 turbos. I got a silver one and Rich got a burgundy one. When they got back to DC we kept in touch."

Cats from New York would bounce out of town and hit Interstate 95 to DC. Dope money there was good and the locals were still naïve to out of towners. New Yorkers hadn't gotten cocky yet or fucked every chick on the block and it was still early in the game as the savvy New Yorkers taught the DC natives the tricks of the hustling trade. The city was wide open for New York hustlers back then and they exploited it.

"I wasn't really the out of town dude that Alpo was. I tried to tell him to stay out of there, but he decided to go." AZ said. Alpo would come back with crazy stories of going to Freekneek and all that. He told his homeboys how sweet it was. Everybody started going out of town after that. The New York dealers saw DC as easy money.

"When he started going to DC, he started getting a lot of money," the Spanish Harlem hustler says. "DC was looking good for him and he was getting money. He had a Bronco and a Blazer. He's coming back and forth from out of town. But he didn't really come Uptown anymore. He brought some of his DC people, Wayne Perry and Wayne's cousin Rayful Edmond to East Rivers back then."

Dapper Dan's Boutique
43 • Dapper Dan's Boutique

Harlem World

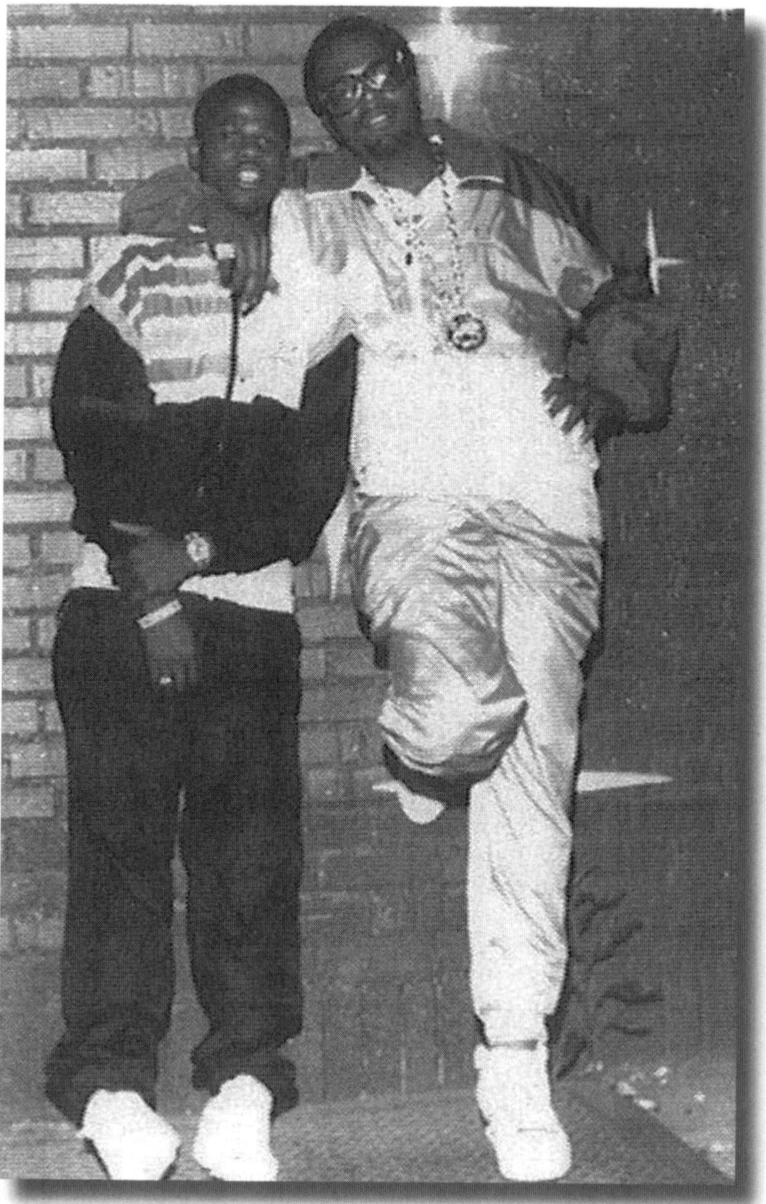

CHAPTER 4
TREACHERY

"Dedicated to Rich Porter's little brother/who died in the struggle/and never got recognized for it." Noreaga, All We Got is Us, Reunion (2000)

The drug game was treacherous. The young princes of Harlem were living the life, but soon it would all come crashing down. "All the thugs, all the homies, all the jacks, they were out to get these guys because they were so young," the Harlem gangster says. "They were living large and flaunting what they had and dudes took notice." The young hustlers were on top, but lots of gun thugs were scheming on their crowns. Because even though they were making plans with their money, others were making plans with their money too.

Disloyalty in the drug game had always existed- greed, envy, lust and hatred made sure of that. Anyone who was trying to become a kingpin was at high risk. "If you had a lot of drug money stashed, somebody would soon be coming for it, especially if the word got out that you were getting money." The East River boriqua says. "You might have had your money on your mind, but somebody else had your money on their mind also."

Alpo, AZ and Rich had targets on their backs from the jump. Their stunting, profiling and ghetto fabulous lifestyles had all the wolves out. They had to stay one step ahead of the game, because one slip up could be detrimental. Alpo knew what time it was. In the ghetto's of Harlem, it was a dog eat dog world. When the mice are shinning, the cats come out to play. Out of the three Alpo knew this best.

He created a lot of beef with his actions, but at the same time he was the type of dude that really and truly did not give a fuck. He was involved in a lot of shoot outs, and if someone popped off at him, he was certain to bust his gun back. Rich was less problematic, but he would also bust his gun with provocation. AZ wasn't really with any of that gun thug, hectic type of shit. He was just trying to eat. But with all the bullets flying, they were bound to catch a few. To what extent, nobody knew.

In the drug game, it was a situation of staying one step ahead of the wolves, but by showing off the trappings of their material success in 24/7, in everybody's face all day, they were tempting fate. That was why AZ had such a big problem with Alpo, he felt he was too flashy. But Alpo was the one busting his gun to watch AZ's back, so what could he really say or do. In AZ's mind, Alpo was a necessary evil.

Alpo went to war also, he didn't shy away from gunplay or beef, he took bullets, and he wasn't naïve when it came to the maxim live by the gun and die by the gun. He participated in many gunfights and was a highly regarded gun thug. He knew the dangers of the street firsthand. He knew that when you lived that type of lifestyle death was always right around the corner. Like a gunslinger from the Wild West, Alpo was more than willing and ready to die. He was more akin to Billy the Kid or Bonnie and Clyde, than a Mafioso.

With the ever present danger of getting caught slipping in mind, Alpo drove a grey bulletproof Porsche. A couple of close calls had him prepared. He knew he had to take preventive measures. He got shot several times, nothing major, but he would step out on the block with a sling on his arm, talking about how a hater shot him. It was just another day in the life of Alpo.

Alpo used to tell dudes, "I gotta pay niggas 10 grand to watch my front and I'll watch my back, but if a muthafucka come at me, he better come correct." Alpo would be clutching a .357 Magnum as he said this, his emphasis clear. Shit got so crazy in the streets of Harlem for Alpo that he tried to ease the pain of his eventual demise for his family. So many dudes were gunning for him at one point that he thought his future death was inevitable.

"Alpo paid a crackhead money one time to call his mom and his sister Monica and say that he had gotten killed because he wanted to spare them," the Spanish Harlem hustler says. "Shit got mad hectic for him in the streets. Dudes had contracts out on him, $10 to $50 g's at a time. Muthafuckas was shooting at him coming out of his moms building, as he was getting in his Jeep."

Alpo would blast back at them. His bullets didn't discriminate. He was armed and ready. Quick to draw and quicker still to pull the trigger. He didn't play around when it came to his life and his gun game was serious. He was a gun thug of epic proportions, but everyone thought he wouldn't last. They figured his days were numbered and there were rumors in the streets that the infamous Preacher was extorting Alpo and Rich. But Alpo disputes this.

"Yeah, let's cover that real quick," Alpo said. "Preacher never took two pennies from me. Preacher never took one penny from Alpo. He would have taken two bullets from me. His situation with Rich was different. Preacher took care of some murders for Rich. Preacher killed a kid named Terry that was his partner. Preacher never came at me with any type of extortion.

"One time Preacher asked me for half a key of coke, but I was in and out of town too much and I never gave it to him. My man that I told you about early from the stick up days (Randy Love), he knew Preacher and he was going to kill Preacher.

Preacher never took anything from me.

"Preacher always thought AZ was a punk; he knew what I was about so he didn't even come at me like that. Him and Rich had an understanding because of Apple being Richard's uncle and Rich paid him $10,000 to kill this kid Sean Mo. They killed him coming off of 145th Street.

"The thing with Preacher, I don't care if it was you talking to Preacher, if people rode by and saw you talking to Preacher, they automatically felt he was getting money from you. That's how strong his rep was for extortion. But anybody that knew me knew I wasn't paying anything. Preacher respected me just like I respected him."

Everyone thought Alpo would get his, but AZ was the first of the trio to get his head knocked, even though Alpo was mainly the one in the line of fire. Word in the streets was that AZ got hit because he didn't have the same amount of respect in the streets for busting his gun that Alpo and Rich had. Stick up artists saw AZ as an easy mark. Plus familiarity breeds contempt and in the streets kindness was always mistook for weakness.

In 1987, a kick door invasion of AZ's stash house left three dead and three others critically injured, including AZ, who was shot nine times, twice in the head at point blank range. It was a vicious attempt to come up, an act of desperation from a hungry wolf, a common event in the drug game. Drug Wars, Five Executed, The New York Post headline read.

"August 20, 1987, that's the day I got shot. They shot like 5 people," AZ said. "The person that set me up was my sister's ex-boyfriend. He was the first person I ever saw smoke crack. He used to keep money. He used to hit me off with shorts when he was messing with my sister- $20, $50 here and there, he got busted for some shit and went to prison. I guess in prison the word was AZ, Alpo and Rich, so when he came home he came to see me. I gave him a brand new Saab convertible.

"At my aunt's apartment in the Bronx, were I used to stash my drugs, I knocked on the door and he opens the door with an Uzi and two other guns. When he opened the door, he grabbed me. I had my man Charlie with me and his girl Lynette with me. They grabbed us and took me to the living room. They took them to the bedroom, where they had my aunt and two of her friends. They took the safe out of the closet and told me to open it.

"Everybody in the bed room was handcuffed. They hit me in the head with a pistol. I was bleeding and shit, trying to open the safe. I was like, 'Yo, Kev' and his man hit me again with a pistol. 'Don't say his name muthafucka, open the safe nigga.' I couldn't open the safe. I got nervous.

"I just said, 'Listen, homie, ain't no money in the safe, but I got like 200 g's at my house. Just don't hurt nobody and y'all can take me to get the money.' Kev whispered something in the guy's ear while he had the Uzi pointed at me. The guy went in the living room and turned up the radio real loud.

"Then the kid came out the back and put the gun to my forehead and pulled the trigger. My Aunt Joan died, my man Charlie died, a friend of my aunt's, Myra Enoch died. Lynette got shot in the head, she lived and my aunt's friend Michael survived gunshot wounds."

AZ survived, but he was in bad shape. He was taken to the hospital, where he and the other two victims of the robbery attempt, were treated. It was a close call and a sobering reality for AZ. The drug game and criminal underworld was vicious. Where enemies were enemies and even friends were potential enemies. And those closest posed the greatest threat of all.

Police stood guard outside his room and members of the press waited out front to interview him. The story made headlines in all the major New York City tabloid newspapers. The news channels gave the story massive airtime also. It was a media free for all that highlighted everything that was wrong in the streets of New York at the height of the crack era. Death, murder, drug addiction and betrayal were the names of the game.

"Neither Rich nor Alpo paid me a visit. But I got a message from them saying they were looking all over for Kevin. I sent a message back telling them to fall back. That the police know everything." AZ said. "After I got shot in the head twice, I had to wake up. They shot me out of the game. The police was all around, they wanted to know who is who."

Despite their man almost getting killed, Alpo and Rich stayed in the game. "When I came home from the hospital in 1987, Rich and Alpo gave me the 411 about the streets," AZ said. "Rich was getting coke from Fritz on 112th Street. They were both making money. Alpo was making regular trips copping bricks in Virginia, Baltimore and DC.

"They gave me the update about new cars they'd copped and the new homes they purchased. I remember both of them sported Rolex watches and nice jewelry. They were getting paid more than ever, going on trips and escorting some beautiful ladies. They'd already ran through all the fly girls in Harlem and became interstate players, transporting girls from different states. The game went on without me and my boys were the talk of the town."

Rich was doing the Harlem thing. Selling jumbos, two for five dollars. He had long lines wrapped around his spots all day and night. "When my crew is out, nobody else gets paid. I got that butter shit," Rich said. He took his cook game serious, just like his gun game, clothes game and money game. Rich Porter always traveled first class. He was an exclusive type of dude where only the best would do.

Rich cooked crack quickly and profited faster than other hustlers. Rich didn't believe in letting anyone else eat. "Fuck that nice guy shit. Nice guys finish last. I need all this paper. I'm not trying to do this shit forever." Rich said. He had one thing on his mind and that was stacking his paper. He was on a mission.

Rich was going hard, but bad luck kept rearing its ugly head. Cops would pull him over, search his ride and take his cash. Deals would go bad and he would lose money. He was taking too many losses. Big amounts at every turn. Rich was taking a lot of hits, but things would go from bad to worse. He just didn't know how bad it would get.

Alpo's life was getting chaotic down in the Chocolate City also. "I ran into Alpo every once in a while and he told me about all the chaos that was coming his way at the time. AZ had been ambushed in the Bronx and shot in the head more than once. I remember AZ when he was younger sitting in the gold Benz with Rich. He was a quiet kid. I don't see why somebody would try to get him like that. Cold blooded." The Uptown player says. "That's just the game treacherous."

A lot of events were happening simultaneously in the streets. The crack epidemic made people crazy and the result was a crime wave that would eventually usher in the War on Drugs and mandatory minimum sentencing guidelines. Everyone was scheming and had their eye on the prize. But they didn't know that only death and prison was in the cards. Alpo and Rich continued on trying to do them, but treachery was everywhere. Rich's prior bad luck would be minor compared to the kidnapping of his brother, an event which ripped his family apart.

Twelve year old Donnell Porter was walking to school alone on a Harlem street when a van screeched to a halt and men wearing masks jumped out of the van and grabbed Donnell. The masked driver opened the door from the inside and Donnell was thrown into the van. The masked men jumped in after him and the van sped off.

Later that afternoon, Donnell's sister Patricia received a phone call from a man saying Donnell had been kidnapped and was being held for ransom. The kidnappers wanted 500 grand and Donnell would be killed if the police were notified or the ransom wasn't paid. Kidnappings of dealers in New York weren't uncommon, but the snatching of a 12 year old moved the practice to a new low.

"They thought because of the fancy cars and jewelry that Rich had it like that, but he didn't. Richard felt like even if they gave up the money, he wouldn't see his little brother again," Patricia Porter said. Rich knew the game was vicious and that snatch artists and stick up kids didn't like to leave any witnesses. That was the law of the jungle.

Since Rich was doing his thing in a big way at the time, there were many who assumed that he possessed multitudes of cash, when in fact he really didn't. In the hood, when people see dealers buying new cars every other week they think the cash flow is endless. Because that's how it seems to someone on food stamps. But Rich was out there hustling and grinding to keep up his fronts. He was living like a millionaire but didn't have a million dollars.

Consequently, it was probably his lifestyle that determined how dudes in the street perceived his wealth, because Rich was turning 30-40 keys a month. However, after buying cars for $70,000 in cash and living in cribs in Jersey, which were being sold for a quarter of a million, he wasn't holding as much cash flow in his stash as it appeared.

"When his little brother got kidnapped he came down the block and you could literally see that he was fucked up. It was written all over his face." The Harlem gangster says. Rich was in dire straits and it all seemed to be crumbling inwardly for him. His life was in a downward spiral and he didn't even realize it.

"When I got there, Rich had arrived and he was visibly upset," AZ said. "His left leg trembled and he kept shaking his head in disbelief. His mother was screaming, 'I hope you don't owe nobody money out there. If you do, you better pay them, because I want my son home now. My son don't got shit to do with this. Nothing better happen to my son.'"

A second call was made and the ransom was lowered to $350 g's. The man on the phone spoke nervously as he demanded the money and instructed the family to go to the restroom of the McDonalds at 125th Street on Broadway in Manhattan. He told them to look under the sink. The kidnappers wanted Rich to know they meant business.

"There's something that will show you just how serious me and my people are." The kidnapper said. In the mid-80s in the kidnapping game some vicious and heinous acts went down, all in the name of the dollar. It was a cold blooded way to get money. The kidnappers would get theirs by any means necessary. The family was warned again not to involve the police and the caller said he'd be in touch. There were several more phone calls made to Rich, but mutually agreeable terms could not be reached.

A Porter family friend went to the McDonald's and checked the stalls to make sure that no one was waiting to ambush him. He noticed a coffee can under one of the sinks and picked it up and looked inside. Inside the can was the severed pinkie finger of Donnell Porter, with a ring on it bearing the initials D.P., accompanied by a cassette tape.

He took what he found back to the Porter family and they listened to the tape. "Mommy, I don't want to die, please help. Tell Richard to give them the money. Mommy, I love you, tell Pat I love her too. Help me. Don't let them kill me. They cutted my finger." Patricia heard this and went crazy. She ran to the cops.

Once Pat involved the police, the incident made the headlines of New York City's tabloid newspapers and the evening news. The FBI got involved and tapped the phones. Once the police were notified, the kidnappers did not contact the family again. The investigators concluded that Donnell being kidnapped and the ransom demands were due to Rich's involvement in the drug trade.

A few days passed with no calls or contact and Rich's uncle, Apple Porter, showed up and had a note that he said was slid under his aunt's door. The note read, He's still alive. We still want the money. He needs to be in a hospital. He lost a lot of blood, he is getting weak. We know the pigs are involved. Be wise. This is your last chance. Go to a phone on the corner of 20th Street and Sherman Avenue, come alone, we will call you at nine o'clock sharp. Apple told Rich to do it, but Rich took the letter and handed it over to the feds.

"I knew Rich and I knew he didn't care about any of them, from his mother to his little brother. If he did, when his brother got kidnapped, he wouldn't have been trying to make a deal about his life." Alpo said. There were hard truths and hard realities in the drug game. Things happen that can never be planned for and how you react in the heat of the moment can define you and your legacy. Pressure busts pipes.

In the streets, the word was that the Preacher did it. They were saying Alpo was putting the Preacher onto people for kidnapping purposes. Rich didn't know what to believe. He was fucked up. He was leery of everyone. He didn't know what to do and he feared his little brother was lost. It was all a little overwhelming for him.

When AZ told Rich to pray to God for his brother, Rich said, "God don't give a fuck about me. The streets took care of me all my life. Not my mother or my father, just me hustling. I've been doing this ever since I was 13 years old. I can't turn back now. Tell God to get my little brother back."

Rich was through with the cops. All they had done was make the situation worse. He was going to try and hustle up the money to get his brother back alive. He got with his man Alpo to make a plan. Hustling was all he knew. It was in his blood. He would go hard or die trying. Long before 50 Cent coined the phrase.

Two detectives pulled up to the corner of 132nd Street, off of 7th Avenue where Rich was talking with Alpo. The detectives began to question the two. After both of their identities were verified, Alpo was allowed to leave and the detectives asked Rich to come with them to the precinct to talk. Rich went with the officers.

The detectives interviewed Rich at the 32nd Precinct on 135th Street, between 7th and 8th Avenues. The detectives told Richard they knew he was a major drug lord. They told him they needed him to cooperate so they could help get Donnell back. Rich stated that he had no idea what was going on or who would do something like that. The investigators tried for weeks to get a lead on the kidnapping, but nothing came up. Time was running out.

Rich was clearly paranoid and nervous. He was strapped and wore a bulletproof vest everywhere he went. He was ready to go to war. He went to see his connect, Richard "Fritz" Simmons. Rich asked Fritz for some money to get his brother back. Fritz tried to talk Rich out of paying any money for a ransom, but he told him he would help him another way.

Fritz took Rich upstairs into his apartment and Rich came down with a Louis Vuitton bag full of keys of coke and took off. Fritz said Rich appeared to be in a daze. Fritz basically gave Rich the keys, because he believed in helping a brother out that was doing bad. Fritz had all the money, but he gave Rich the work to get his brother back. Fritz told Rich, "Just use that to get your brother back, I don't want a dime." Fritz was the king of Manhattan's coke department.

"Fritz told Rich to meet him in Harlem one day and delivered to him about 30 kilos of coke and said, get your brother back and get out of the game." AZ said. Now Rich had the ways and means to make a move to get his little brother back, but he didn't account for someone else's greed. That is something you can never account for in the drug game, where betrayal can happen in a second and loyalty turns to treachery at the sign of a quick come up.

Rich called Alpo to sell the work out of town for him, because he felt he was too hot to move it with all that was going on. The feds and the NYPD had their eyes on Rich. They were watching him for clues to solve the kidnapping. This was a delicate situation for Rich, because the streets were saying Alpo had something to do with the kidnapping. They felt he was in on the move, but Rich trusted his man.

"Rich, being hot by the feds, asked Alpo to move the joints for him. This gave Alpo an opportunity." AZ said. An opportunity to put a snake move down. He had done it before, turning on those who trusted him wasn't new to Alpo, because Alpo cared about one person, Alpo.

"They were accusing me of that when it first happened. They heard someone speaking Spanish on the tape when they sent the finger. So they were like thinking I had something to do with it." Alpo said. "His brother was a cool little kid. He was in the streets too much for his age. Rich had love for his little brother. It just wasn't that tough love. Rich knew he should have kept that little boy off the streets, because Rich was in the streets."

When the feds busted the Preacher crew in August 1996, the story finally came out. Apple Porter, Rich's uncle, was a member of the crew. After he fell out with the crew, he switched sides and confessed to five murders, and told investigators what happened to Donnell Porter, his nephew. It was a story that needed to be told, because for years no one knew what had happened.

Apple told investigators that he and Maalik, another Preacher crew member, put masks and gloves on and abducted Donnell on his way to school. They brought Donnell to a building controlled by the crew. The kidnappers thought Donnell had the key to his mom's house. They figured Rich used his mom's house for a stash pad for money. They planned to get the key from Donnell and ransack the house for money. But Donnell didn't have the key.

Once the kidnappers realized the boy didn't have the key the plan changed. They started making calls to the family demanding the ransom. To let them know they were serious they taped the message from Donnell and cut off his finger. What had started out as one thing, turned into something completely different in the chaos of the moment.

"I knew Preacher," AZ said. "I thought he and Rich's uncle were tight and I thought he would do things for us, instead of doing things to us. That's why you can't show people too much." Things would go from tragic to worse for the Porter family. As they say, when it rains it pours and everything seemed to be happening at once.

"My beeper went off like crazy, displaying 911 on the screen. I knew it was my mom. I jumped out of the car and called her. 'You know they found Pat's brother dead, right?' I had a feeling something happened." AZ said. The inevitable had happened, but it wasn't what AZ thought.

"Pat was in tears when I called her. I knew she was hurting

and I could only imagine how Rich would react when he found out. 'I heard about the bad news, Pat. Did you speak to Rich yet? Does he know about Donnell?' She told me, 'AZ, Richard was killed, not Donnell.'"

Nearly a month after Donnell's kidnapping, Richard Porter's body was found in Pelham Bay Park in the Bronx. He'd been shot in the head and the chest. He still had his jewelry on and a few thousand dollars in cash on him, so robbery was immediately ruled out. This further frustrated the detectives investigating the kidnapping, because they knew that since Richard was dead, Donnell wouldn't be returned.

Everybody was down on the block talking about Rich being killed. When Alpo arrived, he got out of his car crying. "Yo, what happened to Rich? They killed Richard. I can't believe this, somebody got to die." Alpo said and jumped back into his car and took off. But nobody bought his performance. On the block the accusations flew.

"Yo, we got to kill him. Alpo killed Rich. I know you know that. We can't let him get away with killing Rich; he was acting like he didn't even know." They were saying. Nobody trusted Alpo and everyone knew he was a snake. Everyone loved Rich and they wanted to avenge him. Even though it wasn't confirmed, everyone blamed Alpo for Rich's murder.

Alpo was feeling the heat heavy in Harlem. He even asked dudes, "Do you think if I give them 50 grand each do you think they'll stop saying that." Alpo didn't like being blamed for Rich's murder. It was an accusation he couldn't abide. The innuendo and rumor ate at him, damaging his status in Harlem and in the streets.

The detectives hit the streets hard and pulled in anybody associated with Richard Porter. The kidnapping and murder, back to back, had to be solved. There were several arrests made, and all the people arrested were questioned about the murder of Richard and the kidnapping of Donnell. But nobody knew what was up, it was all speculation. But detectives thought the two acts were connected.

An informant, threatened with being taken down for the distribution of narcotics began to talk, he stated, "Maybe it was one of the big drug dealers Richard owed money to. I don't know. Maybe it was Alpo or John-John or Lou from 142nd Street, maybe it was Preacher." But after bringing in several individuals, on mostly petty charges, the police were still no closer to figuring out the case than they were from the first day. That didn't keep the streets were talking. But no one knew the whole truth until later.

When the Preacher crew went down in 1996, different details about the events emerged. Rich's uncle told investigators that he wanted to take what his nephew Rich Porter had built while he was in prison. Apple said Rich wouldn't allow him to be a part of his operation. Apple promised Preacher half, then Preacher and Apple agreed to grab Donnell. Apple also said that when he found out that Richard was killed he talked to Preacher, and they both realized the ransom would not be paid.

Alpo never came back around; he didn't attend Rich's wake or the funeral. He was too busy going out of town selling drugs. Plus with everyone in the streets blaming him for the kidnapping and murder, implying he had something to do with it, he wasn't a very popular figure in Harlem. Out of everything that happened, the stain on his reputation was what he couldn't stand the most. Alpo's street fame was everything to him.

"When the Rich Porter thing happened, everybody was kind of fucked up behind that, because niggas had love for him in Harlem and everywhere in the city," the East River boriqua says. "Dudes knew that Alpo had something to do with that because he was a stick up kid from the very beginning. So you know that mentality never really leaves you, and when you start out sticking people up, taking what you want, every situation you are confronted with, that doesn't go your way, that survival skill surfaces, because it's something you know how to do.

"So muthafuckas were whispering that Alpo had something to do with it. Everybody's mindset was not to trust no one, because if the nigga that everybody loved just got bodied by his so called homie, it could happen to anybody." From the jump Alpo was the prime suspect, in the eyes of the streets. Even though the police didn't know the deal, the streets did.

"This was not even a month after Donnell was kidnapped. They said they had the body of Richard." Patricia Porter said. "Richard's dead, we are hoping they send Donnell home. I saw Alpo on 127th and 8th Avenue and Alpo couldn't even look me in the face. My mother said from day one that Alpo killed my son." Rich's mom had a lot to say about the death of her son.

"From the birth of the union between Alpo and my beloved Rich I knew that Alpo would be the Judas who would betray his name, love and friendship and honor. I can understand to some degree, because Alpo always tried to emulate Rich and walk in his shadows. The protégé will always harbor hostilities toward his guide, because it is the guide that commands the attention without even trying, Alpo could never be Rich. A coward dies a thousand times, a soldier dies but once," Velma said. Others were confused by Alpo's alleged actions.

"The Alpo I knew loved Rich. He loved AZ, he loved Harlem." AZ said. "Alpo never did no sheisty shit to me or Rich, so when that happened it hurt. I was like who are you? I will never try to dis him, but why? A lot of them who were trying to dis him were happy that shit happened because that dynasty was crazy. I know if he could rewind his mind back and see how Rich could enjoy it with us. He would've done that."

Less than a month after Rich's murder, another body was found in the same Bronx park. It was the body of a small black male, frozen and wrapped in more than a dozen plastic bags. Investigators noticed right away that the child was missing a finger. It was Rich Porter's little brother.

"Okay, now we know," Patricia said. "His body was pretty well preserved. They had him in the freezer." Dudes were heartbroken when they heard the news about Donnell. Harlem was in shock. First Rich, then his little brother. It was the end to a chapter. A tragic crack era, drug game story that showed all the worst aspects of humanity.

The Porter family was notified that a body fitting Donnell's description had been found and that they needed to come down to identify the remains. After Donnell's family identified him at the morgue, the medical examiner determined that the boy was killed by blunt force trauma to the head. The kidnappers had smashed in Donnell's small skull. A brutal and unfitting end to a young life.

The medical examiner also determined that Donnell was alive when his finger was cut off. The medical examiner could not determine whether the body was kept in a freezer or if it had frozen from the extremely cold weather. Allegedly, Preacher told Apple that Donnell saw their faces so he had to die- ransom or no ransom. That was just the way it went down in the criminal underworld, no witnesses.

After the Preacher crew bust in 1996, Apple told the investigators that it was Maalik who actually killed Donnell, as well as being the one that cut his pinkie off. But Maalik was already dead by this time, so there was no way to verify his story. Regardless of his cooperation with authorities, Apple went to prison for life, and rightly so. He played a part in a very evil deed.

"It was unbelievable. What really hurt was their own family did it to them. Rich was killed by Alpo and Donnell by his own uncle. They were all good people, but that transformation is a muthafucka for that dollar," AZ said. "I wasn't with all that killing and crazy stuff. Donnell was the lamb of the whole situation. Two days after his funeral a big rainbow came over 32nd Street and 7th Avenue where we used to hang out. Nothing that happened to me, Rich and his little brother came from the outside it came from the inside."

Shit went crazy after Alpo killed Rich. He denied left and right that he did it. He would sing that song to anyone who would listen. But the truth was Alpo thought Rich and AZ were blackballing him. AZ told Alpo they didn't have any work, and then Rich came up with the bag of keys from Fritz. Alpo let paranoia rule his mind and his actions.

"I feel like what he did the devil made him do it. A lot of the things cats did in this game, the devil made them do it," AZ said. Eventually Alpo admitted to killing Rich. Alpo shot Rich on January 3, 1990. He gave his reasons in a F.E.D.S. magazine interview and he seemed to regret it, but what's done was done.

"Definitely killing Rich, if I could change that I would. I would change the murders." Alpo said. "Why did I kill Rich, it wasn't personal, it was business. Rich was lying to me about something he shouldn't have been. I gave him the opportunity to tell me the truth, not once but twice. I am truly sorry to the Porter family." But that can't change what he did.

"Of course Alpo couldn't say, 'I killed him for greed.' He had to make the streets accept it with a seemingly legitimate claim or allegation. The streets don't lie and they see right through your justification for killing him for those 30 kilos." Velma said, Rich's mom countered. But Alpo kept trying to justify the murder.

"The reason I killed Rich," Alpo said. "I killed Rich, because I had a young Dominican connect off Broadway who wasn't really in the position at the time I was dealing with him, to really front me crazy bricks. He would front me one or two, but he wasn't in the position to front me 60 or 100 keys. We didn't want to put up the money, we wanted him to front us and we would put up half the money. Since my connect couldn't do it, Rich used a kid from the Bronx that was hitting him lovely.

"Then it stopped, the kid caught a dry spell. So since I was going out of town I told Rich, even though I never met your connect, I'm going to introduce you to my connect. What I said was, 'You take your money and I'll give you my money. Take care of it. Deal with your connect or mine.'

"I didn't mind if Rich made $1,000 a brick off me with his man. I was coming with about 400 or 500 grand at a time. At the time my connect was sometimes cheaper, he's giving Rich the joints for an even cheaper price. Let's say he gave Rich 100 keys, 50 of them were for me. He'd give them to Rich. Rich never tells me about my connect.

"One day I'm in New York, looking for this kid that ran off with about 190 g's. I run into my connect. I ask him when he's going to start looking out for us. He had a lot of respect for me and I had a lot of respect for him too. He tells me he just gave Rich 60 joints and 30 were mine. I said, 'No, you didn't.'

"So he describes them to me. I remember they had a president's name on them and the box they came in. I told him not to say anything about it. I take my bricks back down to DC that I had just got from Rich and went to my man Gary's.

"Me and Gary had become like me and Rich in NY. Gary was my man in DC. He was also my best customer and he was about his murder game. I went back and told Gary what Rich did. He knew who Rich was because I took Gary with me to New York before. The first thing that comes out of his mouth is, 'Let's kill him.'

"I was like hold up for a minute, let me think about it. I called Rich and asked him. 'Is everything alright? Is your man back?' He said, 'Yeah, my man just gave me some more joints, you coming up?' I said, 'Yeah, I was there.' I hung up the phone and told my little man we're going to New York to see Rich.

"I went to New York and spent about $500 g's with Rich. At this time he was getting bricks from Fritz. I take the coke back to DC and me and my man come back to New York. I said, 'I'm going to ask him one more time who he's getting his coke from. If he lies I'm going to take him out.'

"One thing led to another and I killed Rich. Rich lied to me about something there was no reason to lie about. If that little bit of money can come between what I thought was a wonderful relationship, there's no telling what he might do down the line. I gave him the opportunity to tell me the truth, not once, but twice.

"Gary shot him, I think two times and he didn't die, so I shot him. I would like to say I got my money back from Rich. No question. Like I said, I had just spent money with Rich and he hit me with some joints, so I just kept them. Once you take care of that first murder in your life, you're alright. Not that I'm saying it's a good thing. I was doing what I had to do."

Alpo killed Rich Porter and ended their friendship permanently. After murdering his best friend in cold blood, Alpo had to bounce, because Rich Porter was beloved in Harlem and the streets were out for Alpo's head. Suspicion was growing as to his role in the murder, and eventually someone would get it in their mind to finish Alpo to avenge Rich.

Alpo had his reasons for killing Rich, but everyone in Harlem believed Alpo killed Rich for the 30 keys Fritz gave him. The bricks that were meant to help Rich raise the ransom for his kidnapped brother. In the eyes of the streets that was sacrilege. That's why Alpo was vilified in Harlem. He represented the worst kind of evil in the drug game. It was supposed to be death before dishonor, but Alpo destroyed the romantic notion of honor among thieves.

The majority of Alpo's business dealings outside of New York were centralized around Virginia Beach and Washington, DC. It didn't matter if he couldn't hustle in Harlem, he was still Alpo. When dudes had beef in the city and it was hard for them to stay in town, they just went out of town to get money. That was how the New York hustlers did it and Alpo was already established. Back in Harlem, the streets wept.

"All that I had- the cars, the jewelry, the furs- I would give it all up if I could get my brothers back." Patricia said. As Alpo hustled in DC, Harlem came to grips. The loss of Rich Porter to the injustices of the drug game, spawned a monumental legend that has lived on. The event also played a major part in Alpo's history and how he's perceived today. The murder of his partner, Rich Porter, is something he will never live down.Sadly, the treacherous act has come to define him.

CHAPTER 5

WASHINGTON, DC

"And Alpo ordered guys to slaughter guys/and the whole Harlem was in tears when Rich Porter died."
Cam'Ron, I Remember When, Children of the Corn (2003)

Washington, DC was synonymous with the crack era in the late-80s. The easily marketed, easily ingested cocaine rolled down in cars from New York to our nation's capital and by 1986, crack roots had grown deep and strong. Crack found a fertile and virgin market in DC and New York dealers preyed on the openness of the city with their big city charms. To the New York hustlers, DC was sweet.

As they flooded the city with crack cocaine every aspect of life in Washington, DC was shaped by the tiny rock. It revolutionized DC's robbers, hardened its dealers and transformed its cops. The drug tarnished DC's public image, manipulated its health care economy, dominated its politics and influenced its residential patterns. If one city became a symbol of the crack scourge, it was Washington, DC.

Crack quickly became the most popular drug on the block

and its effects were immediate- home robberies, crack babies, carjackings, shootings, kidnappings, homelessness- DC was awash with chaos, violence and mayhem, all generated by crack. As the city became the murder capital of the world by any means necessary quickly became the M.O. and the local ghettos became a playground for out of state gun thugs.

New York hustlers made DC their second home. They flocked to the city. During the late-80s DC was a gold mine for New Yorkers selling crack. The economy in DC was earning New York hustlers' top dollar for their product. A gram of crack that went for $20 in New York, sold for $100 in DC. With the economics in place and money to be made, New York dealers swarmed DC.

"The mentality of a New Yorker going out of town and getting money is pretty simple," the East River boriqua says. "Back then we could get just about any drug cheaper than most states and we didn't have to search far to get them. We can sometimes double or triple our money when we go out of town depending on what we were taking out there." Taking drugs out of town became a rite of passage for a New York drug dealer.

The urban tales being brought back to New York from DC made it seem like hustling in DC was easy money. But Washington DC, at this time, was a virtual war zone. The drug trade bred killers and the streets of the Chocolate City learned quickly. DC soldiers went hard, and DC became dangerous and violent virtually overnight.

As New York hustlers continued migrating down to DC to make paper, DC hustlers took the welcome signs down. But when DC hustlers needed coke, they looked to New York dudes as connects, allowing them to get in position. It was a situation of supply and demand and once the New York dealers showed the DC dudes the game, they wanted it all for themselves. But they knew that without a connect they were hit.It was all supply ad demand.

The drug economy in DC was so attractive because dealers in DC didn't have any direct drug connections for the most part.

Only Rayful Edmond established a source which didn't involve New Yorkers. All the rest of the coke in the city was coming down from the Big Apple. Interstate-95 was the drug pipeline that fed our nation's capital. And dealers like Alpo capitalized on this fact.

"Many New Yorkers believe that if they can make paper in New York City, than they can definitely get paid out of New York City." The East River boriqua says. "The city life comes at you fast and there's always something to be on the lookout for from the cops, to stickup kids, to the niggas that just want to make a name for themselves by pushing a nigga's head back that's making noise. There's always that thought that niggas from New York City were faster on their toes."

This led to an emerging arrogance in New York gun thugs. They thought that other city's gangsters were slow. That they could get over on them. But often times the New Yorkers worked with the locals. "A New York dude would go down there and put the DC guys to work," the Harlem gangster says. "It worked both ways."

The drug economy was good to the native DC dealers too. Being fed kilo's of crack was creating DC drug tycoons. That's why they allowed the New Yorkers to come through whole-saling and setting up shop. It was all a means to an end. One hand looks out for the other.A mutual business venture and understanding.

"The economy was crazy down there," the Harlem player says. "We were getting five times the money we would up in New York. We had blocks poppin' down there. There was coke everywhere because of New York niggas. We could afford to flood the streets like that. One kilo of cocaine could make you the man in DC at this time." With continued success, more dealers flooded the streets of DC with coke.

"I think personally that the opportunity might present itself more to someone in New York City because almost everyone that was hustling back then knew that their rainbow started in New York City, and with some luck and the right connect, ended in their state paid in full," the East River boriqua says. "Another thing was the fact that when dudes went out of town they used fake names, kind of giving them a pass to get buck wild out there if you had to, because no one really knows who you are. The M.O. was get money, cause havoc and roll back to New York City where you were safe and no one knew what you were doing."

In 1987, Alpo stopped going Uptown so much. He was making good money taking loads down to DC. "Alpo started getting some money in DC. He hooked up with Rayful Edmond and then moved on to the notorious Wayne Perry, Big Head Gary and Little Pop, among other DC criminals. I remember Alpo coming back to the city bragging, 'I just made about 300 grand and change in four days, nigga.'" AZ said.

Alpo wasn't doing anything new. He was just following the money and bringing his New York style to the Chocolate City. Most New Yorkers considered DC dudes bamma's, they thought they were slow and countrified. They found the city easy and the locals open. They took advantage of the situation that presented itself. It was a crack bonanza.

"We came down there and ended up fucking all their broads, had their people working for us, we taking care of the neighborhood." The Uptown player says. "A lot of beef came from the fact that we were just so different. It was like being from two different cultures. DC did the go-go thing and New York the rap thing. We were wearing Dapper Dan's and they were wearing the latest gear from the Madness shop. We were bound to clash, but there was too much money involved and DC was too small." It was a combustible juxtaposition.

"Harlem became a headache for me, so I went down to DC with this girl Karen." Alpo said. "I put my jewelry together and I go on down. I'm in DC getting familiar with everybody. The girl Karen knows everybody and everybody knows her, because she used to mess with some serious ballers in that town.

"Come to find out, they think I'm the police down there. She takes me to a place called the Florida Avenue Grill, where everyone would go to eat, and if you were a baller you would get your car washed. All these people are trying to find out who I was. Niggas start whispering and she had an uncle that found out they thought I was a federal agent.

"This kid I used to look up to on the Eastside is down there, he is running with a kid named Mike Fray, an older cat. Mike was real strong in DC. People had a lot of respect for him. So this kid is with Mike Fray and he starts kicking my name around and lets dudes know I am just trying to do my thing. Everybody knows I'm not an agent." Alpo was free to do business in DC.

"Alpo's first connection to DC was when he met Karen in Virginia Beach," a local dude from the era we'll call Spud says. "In Virginia Beach at the time they used to have the black student beach week type of thing. It was at the end of the school year. They ended up meeting there and a couple of weeks later Alpo invited Karen and Kim up to New York. They went up and hung out with Alpo and Rich and all them and a couple of weeks later Alpo came down.

"I was the third or fourth person to meet Alpo when he came down to DC. He was over at the house chilling, just a fun outgoing dude. Playing basketball for like $500 a game. He came down and had the Mercedes with the seats all decked out from Dapper Dan's and when he first came out the DC ballers used to go to a bowling alley and bowl and Alpo was coming out in his Gucci and MCM jackets and a lot of people thought he was the feds.

"What happened was Fray talked to Red Jack and said 'Who is this guy?' Red Jack was an older dude from New York who told Fray that Alpo was legit. Fray used to fuck with Red Jack, who was from Harlem and Alpo knew Red Jack from New York. Alpo just got in with everyone after that coming back and forth. He was just about making money. He was making connections and actually at the time Fray and him were really cool with each other. They were cool.

"He wasn't bring down big loads at first because Rayfu still had the town on lock. Po was doing his thing dibbling and dabbing, maybe doing five keys here or ten there. At first there was no need for him because Ray had the connect. Nobody's connect could hang with Rays connect at that time."

"Ray and Po met and Ray was cool with Alpo. Ray wasn't really a gangster he was just a guy who was about making money. He just got to big and what they made him out to be wasn't him. When the coke went to crack that is when the bodies started dropping."

Alpo was making inroads and getting established at the same time Rayful Edmond got busted. With Rayful out of the picture Alpo filled the vacuum left in the coke trade. It was a simple case of being the right person in the right place at the right time and capitalizing on it. Alpo wasn't naïve and he knew how to put a move down on multiple levels.

"He was getting keys for like 16 and selling them for 24 or breaking it down and cooking it into crack. He was probably getting 32-36 grand on that. In the city, we were getting 5,000 lean back on 125 grams, so I know they were getting way more than that in DC. Not to mention if you sell it straight up in powder, it's less than if you sell it cooked." The East River boriqua says.

"When he started going to DC, crack was taking over everywhere. Everyone literally knew what crack was, crack was at that point, so the money might have been the main reason the nigga went out of town, because you were going to take the same chances out in New York City that you would in another state, but the pay was twice the money." Plus with his problems in Harlem, hustling in DC was a better option for Alpo.

"He came down to DC. Ray was in, so there was no coke in the city, niggas was fucked up. So Alpo came and if you presenting coke at a good price then they bought from him." Twala McClain, Wayne Perry's girlfriend said. "That's why DC clung on to Alpo, because Ray was gone, Ray held DC down. Ray was the one supplying and everybody knew Ray held DC down. So when Ray left, that's when Alpo came. I don't believe that Alpo would have started his thing if Ray was still there, he wouldn't have been able to, there would have been no room for him."

Alpo was a go-between for dudes from DC looking to cop after Rayful got indicted and convicted. Alpo moved his operations to DC just at the right time. There was an opening in DC and he came in and got it done. He had the correct accolades on his resume and filled the position of drug lord that Rayful vacated.Thats what happens in the drug game.

"I give the nigga Po a lot of credit for getting money like he was," the Uptown player says. "Getting on I95 and flooding DC. He got a lot of money, he was making 300, 400 grand at a time in DC. He would get triple what he could in New York. All the work was coming out of New York. The Dominicans ran that shit out of Washington Heights." With his connections in the cocaine world, Alpo knew DC was a gold mine.

"I was seeing about $6,000 off every brick. I'm a wholesaler," Alpo said. "I would go to DC with 30 bricks and sell them all in one day. I had 10 to 15 good customers and I was giving it to them at a good price. If someone in DC had them for 21 or 22 I was giving them up for 18, so I wound up meeting some other cats like Curtbone and Rayful Edmond. Rayful was like one of the biggest cats coming out of DC, when he went to jail, I really took over the town. A lot of dudes started coming to me." Alpo put himself in position to take over the town.

"He learned DC better than DC niggas," the Uptown player says. "He was bailing dudes out of jail. Hitting them off. He helped a lot of niggas out." Alpo was using all his charm and charisma to win over the local dealers, but in reality the quality and price of the coke was the main reason he got in position so fast. His business acumen enabled him to make serious paper in a relatively short amount of time.

"Alpo was coming back to the city, pulling up in big body Benz's, Porsches, BMW's, bikes, trucks, limos, all kinds of cars and of course flashy as ever with the jewelry." The East River boriqua says. "Everybody in the city was talking about how Alpo was going out of town to DC and selling work. The talk was cocky at times like when niggas wanted to kiss his ass they would bring it up when he was present on how he went out there and locked it down and was killing it, both with drugs and the work he was putting in."

Alpo was spreading the love and getting dudes on his team, but still the stick up kids were after him. "DC dudes are quick with their guns and they will kill you in a minute, especially if they think you are from out of town." Alpo said. "I got shot because they were trying to kidnap me in DC. Only thing that saved me was I looked over my shoulder. I saw four dudes coming to get me and I started running."

Alpo was loud and acted like a clown at times. This attracted the wrong kind of attention. He liked to play the slip game and was the type of person that could never be trusted, but he had good survival instincts and with his concern of looking out for himself first, he stayed one step ahead of the gun thugs. But he knew he had to change his game up or he would wind up dead. He needed an equalizer.

"When Alpo got shot he was on the machine. It was breathing for him. It changed him. He knew he had to step his game up. Alpo said killers respect killers. Drugs and murder went together. If he didn't have that killer attitude, he would have been hit. I think going out of town is what transformed Alpo. I guess he had to lay down his murder game out there and do whatever he had to do to survive, but in Harlem he was loved." AZ said.

Alpo was known for his flash and style in Harlem, but in DC he became a cocaine kingpin that left a trail of bodies behind him. After he was shot, he was introduced to Wayne Perry, the notorious DC hit man, and the two teamed up, to cement their legacies in the streets. It was a vicious combination that would once again turn treacherous. Because Alpo could never stay loyal, it just wasn't in his nature.

CHAPTER 6

THE COME UP

"Uptown was Alpo, Son, heard he was kingpin, yo." Nas, Memory Lane, Illmatic (1994)

Wayne Perry was in one word, notorious. Alpo knew it and he knew if he got Wayne Perry on his team it was over. Alpo's only competition had been Rayful Edmond, and when he went to prison, Alpo took over the town. But he knew he needed an enforcer to keep the wolves at bay.

Wayne Perry had the city on lock with the fear game and was putting the press down on every dealer in the city. With Alpo's need for a bodyguard, so that he could move around the city unmolested, Wayne fit the bill. It was a mutually beneficial relationship. Both sides saw advantages to the partnership.

Wayne saw a golden opportunity in dealing with Alpo, at a time when coke was short in the city, so Wayne took Alpo under his wing. He would keep him close and it was a win-win situation for both. At the time, it seemed a match in gangster heaven, a drug dealer found his enforcer and vice versa. Wayne was a frequent visitor to jail, due to his gun play, and that was how Alpo got to him.

"I met my little man Pop, through some other cats and he was a young, wild 15 year old kid, coming out of Southeast DC, killing anything moving. He just wanted to be under somebody that was going to look out for him, so I wound up taking him under my wing and looking out for him," Alpo said.

"Things started getting a little crazy for me. Through him, I met another cat named Wayne Perry. Now this kid here, he had the town locked on fear and was putting his murder game down. Anyone that mentioned his name, mentioned murder in the same sentence, because he was about his work and didn't have no problem telling everybody, because if you tried to tell or testify he was getting at you.

"The kid Wayne wound up going to jail for a murder and no one was trying to get him out. The people he thought were going to get him out and come up with the money never came up with it. The young kid Pop wound up stepping to me like, 'Yo, my man is in jail.' My man had an uncle that knew him and my little man had a reputation for being wild and about his business. His bail was like $10,000 but I saw the bigger picture.

"I knew if I get this kid out with the reputation he has, all that will come on my side. I wound up giving the whole ten and it was ten well worth it. I got him out. I just let it be known through my little man. Wayne knew what my little man was about and killers respect killers and we became real tight.

"At first I got a lot of negative feedback, people were like, 'We aren't really trying to mess with you.' Because a lot of dudes were scared of this dude, but getting him out with the reputation he had would be good for me. He sent the message that he was there if I needed him.

"The kid was a real good, loyal dude and he really respected that I got him out and he felt like he owed me. One thing led to another and he handled the security aspect of it. He became like my lieutenant, he didn't handle the drugs.

"If you were a customer of mine, you dealt with me. I didn't need anyone else, but if it came a time to put the murder game down, because someone was getting disrespectful or trying to come at me, that's when he stepped in.

"Now with my New York reputation and Wayne, I had the town locked down, they knew we were dangerous. That's how I became real strong in DC. I had that small town on lock for a good period. We went at a lot of dudes that were holding it down." But Wayne Perry had a different take on the hook up.

"I met Po in 89. I was out to destroy him over a lie a girl told me he said. I didn't know him and he was scared to death, but he was with Ray's close comrade Lil' Pop, who asked me not to kill Po." Wayne said.

With Wayne on his team, Alpo took over DC. Since Rayful was out of the picture, Alpo became the biggest source for kilos in the area. It was a natural progression. As soon as one big dealer goes to prison another one steps in to fill his shoes. In the drug game there was always opportunity, and opportunity favored a prepared mind. There was no luck about it.

"Alpo had certain power, because Alpo had money. Alpo was like introduced to Wayne by fear, he felt if he could come down here and get Wayne on his team he could run DC and that's what the fuck he did." Twala said. "Back in the day Wayne got locked up and needed some bail money and a lot of dudes didn't want to put up the bail money because they didn't want to see Wayne back out on the street.

"There was a little dude named Pop. Wayne was like his uncle, he was a little dude, but he just didn't give a fuck. Pop went to Po and told him that his uncle needed money to get out of jail. Po was familiar with Wayne and his motives was like if, 'I can get this nigga out I can have him on my team.' Po put up 10 g's supposedly but let Wayne tell it, that's not how it went down. Wayne said that nigga didn't put up that much money, somebody else did. When he got out, Wayne and Alpo collaborated and they started doing business.

"They hooked up and that's how Wayne started the hit man thing, but he was already doing his thing. The team play was Alpo had the drugs. Wayne never sold drugs, that wasn't his thing. Wayne took what he wanted, Wayne extorted. Alpo knew that, so Alpo had the drugs, Alpo had the money, Wayne had money, but Alpo had more money. So Wayne felt he could get things done with Alpo.

"A lot of murders was committed simply over pussy and over bitches. Alpo needed Wayne. He knew if he had Wayne niggas wouldn't rob or try him, because he knew he was a bitch ass nigga, and if niggas knew that Wayne was behind him niggas would be petrified. Alpo had the money and Wayne had the power." And Wayne put Alpo into power through the murders and body counts.

"When Po hooked up with Wayne that was the best thing that ever happened to him. Po had the money and the coke. Wayne had the power. If you wasn't on their team then watch out," the Spanish Harlem hustler says. "Wayne Perry did not make Alpo who he was, but when Alpo went to DC, that was a different story. If you got something from Alpo and didn't return it then Wayne was gonna come see you and most likely he was going to kill you. Alpo ended up taking over DC because he had Wayne Perry. He was trying to

lock down all DC and the Potomac region."

During his time supplying DC's narcotics market, its estimated Alpo was taking in $1 million a month. "Alpo was in DC buying yachts and jewels for his wife and bitches," AZ said. It's said that the music producer, Teddy Riley, bought Alpo's house off him in Virginia Beach during this time. Alpo was part of the in crowd and he moved in the circles of the newly rich and infamous. His presence was in high demand. He was a celebrity in his own right.

"The fucking house that Teddy Riley lives in on Virginia Beach was Alpo's," the Spanish Harlem hustler says. Alpo was balling out of control with Wayne Perry on his team, but he still had problems. Wayne's protection was supposed to make Alpo off limits to the wolves of the city, but they still went at him. When a hustler is shining as brightly as Alpo was, it's open season.

"A lot of people were starting to say they needed to get the kid Po, because he's getting too much money and he's not from here. I got shot because they were trying to kidnap me in DC," Alpo said. "My man Gary, he was getting money. He was really holding, he was one of my best customers. He had a beef with another crew and we couldn't really get at them because they knew us and how we were coming. We had to hire an ally and this kid volunteered, but he wound up being a statistic.

"The day I met him at the car wash, they had other plans, they were going to try and kidnap me. I got shot in my ribs. The only thing that saved me was, as I'm talking to this dude he looks over my shoulder. I follow his eyes and when I turn back he's pulling out his gun. I started running and bullets hit me in the back." That was when Alpo decided to really put Wayne in effect.

"That's when I knew I had to really make my security strong." Alpo said. "Wayne was already there, but that's when I said it's time to just bring him closer, because he knew everybody that was about that conniving, ki1 1ing people for this and for that." To deter the wolves Alpo had to set his own wolf loose.

"Po was meeting someone and they were trying to snatch him," Spud says. "Thats when he got shot. They were trying to kidnap him. Thats pretty much when his demeanor changed. Po said fuck it. I'm not being nice to anybody anymore. If you owe me money Wayne is gonna deal with it and thats when shit really started getting crazy." But Alpo always knew that Wayne could turn on him, that was what he did, rob drug dealers.

"I had trust for Wayne, but the less he knew about where my stashes were and where I was keeping my money the better. I always said, 'I'm worth more to him alive than dead,' because if he doesn't know where the money is or the stash is, why would he want to bring harm to me when I'm feeding him.

"Then there was a thing going around like, 'If you go get coke from Po, after you get the coke, he puts the kid Wayne on you.' But they were just doing that because they were scared of him and they were upset to see him out of jail.

"There was an incident where a guy commented on my trust

in Wayne, while Wayne was there. I told Wayne what he'd said and Wayne just walked over and shot him right in the head, no questions." Wayne Perry was about his business and he stepped up and put in work whenever the need arose. In the process, he dared the whole city to try and fuck with Alpo. Wayne put Alpo on John Gotti status.

Living like an untouchable, Alpo was allegedly moving 30 bricks of coke a day and Wayne was eating like a king. If dudes owed Alpo money and were playing games about paying, Wayne went to get the money and didn't care about who the dude was supposed to be. Wayne Perry didn't take no shorts. He got it how he lived and wasn't anything soft going on with him.

One of the city's biggest drug dealers allegedly owed Alpo close to a million dollars. Alpo wasn't pressing the situation, but Wayne stepped to dude and told him, "That money you owe Po ain't Po's money no more, it's mine and I want that." It's said Wayne had the money the next day and kept it for himself.

In a short time after hooking up with Wayne, Alpo had a ghetto pass and could roam DC safely selling coke, fucking bitches and getting money. He was worth more to Wayne alive than dead. Even the notorious hit man realized this and used it to his advantage. As the money began to pile up, more bodies began to drop.

"Up in New York, there was talk about the kid Perry really being the one putting in the work and holding Alpo down." The East River boriqua says. "So there was both sides of the story running about the city, because there were other dudes from New York City hustling out in DC at the same time as Alpo." And in street circles, the legend and gossip surrounding Alpo was growing. Rich Porter was dead, but Alpo was still chasing his cocaine dreams.

CHAPTER 7

MURDEROUS REIGN

"I'm rich like Porter/havin' Alpo nightmares." The Game, Money L.A.X. (2008)

With Wayne Perry, his enforcer, killing at his command, Alpo murdered his way to the top of the DC cocaine hierarchy. It was a cutthroat business and Alpo was vicious with it. His team was on one million and backing all his plays. "Alpo had DC's best killers- Wayne Perry, Michael Jackson, Little Pop- it was said these niggas had niggas shooting themselves." AZ said.

Alpo started bringing the DC dudes to Harlem to settle his beefs. Alpo was bringing them to Harlem and getting Wayne Perry's hitters to hit dudes in the city he wanted dead. Alpo had scores to settle and killing became the name of the game. As time went on, the money and murder became a blur. It became so normal, it was routine.

At the same time, the FBI and DC homicide detectives were hearing the name Wayne Perry in connection with too many murders. The heat was on and law enforcement went after Wayne, but Wayne and his team put an end to investigations and court cases by putting an end to the witnesses. This was the standard operating procedure for the crew- no witness equaled no case. It didn't matter who was snitching, Wayne would silence them.

"This female in DC was giving information to the police about certain individuals." Alpo said. "She was trying to testify against Wayne. The girl started getting high and one night we were in Southwest around 3 a.m. Here she come skipping down the alley to get some crack. Wayne saw her and sent one of his men to cut her off.

"When she got there he put her in a dope fiend yoke and put her to sleep. They backed a hooptie into the alley and threw her in the backseat. At the time I was asleep in Wayne's MPV. They woke me up and said,'We got her and nobody saw us.' I jumped in my Mustang.

"Wayne gave the keys to the MPV to his girlfriend and told her to follow us. Wayne's thing was also mental torture. He wanted his girlfriend to see him kill this girl in case she ever got any ideas. I'm driving behind Wayne when you see the girl in the backseat come to. Wayne puts a tape in the cassette player and blasts A Bitch is a Bitch by Easy E. The girl comes to and realizes she's in the car with the man that's about to kill her.

"He begins to stab her. First in the face and head and then her body. Then he shot her four or five times. After he did that to her we left her on 295. She was one of the second girls we left on that highway. This girl was ready to testify against him. He beat the case." Murdering women wasn't routine, but the crew would do what they had to do. Most of the time though these hustlers and gun thugs were running up in women.

Alpo was a serial womanizer and he would go to any means to get what he wanted. "He loved pussy to a fault." The Uptown player says. "He was always telling a story about this dude whose girl he wanted, so they caught dude playing ball and while Alpo was shaking hands with dude he had his boy shoot him in the head. Just so Po could fuck his girl.

"He loved to talk about the boat he had or whatever else he had or what he took from dudes, the control he had over dudes who would do whatever he said. The guy Wayne was like his attack dog according to him. Alpo talked about how dumb dudes were to do what he said." It was all a power play to Alpo.

"He had Domenico Benson from Brooklyn killed at a DC basketball game over his wife," AZ said. Alpo had a girl from Brooklyn, who he considered his wife. Domenico used to fuck with her before and when he kept stepping to her Alpo got jealous and had him killed. Alpo didn't play when it came to females.

"Domenico was a situation where he disrespected himself and other people," Alpo said. "That's what happened to him. He thought he was stronger than he really was. I was shaking his hand when I had it done. I didn't care about that. They hit him up close. They walked right up and put the barrel to his forehead and blasted him in broad daylight, right after a basketball game. I had just finished playing basketball in a basketball tournament.

"I didn't play with those Brooklyn dudes. I knew some cool ones that came out of Brooklyn, but I just always remember as a kid how Brooklyn used to like to rob you. So that kind of like stuck with me." Old grudges died hard and Alpo was the type of dude that couldn't let anything go. When murder was on Alpo's mind, he was vicious with it.

"We killed someone over Gary's wife, this kid Andre," Alpo said. "Andre was a good customer. He spent like 400 g's a month with me. I meet Andre's girl and started fucking her, the pussy was good, he found out I was messing with his girl, but he never said nothing. I bought her parent's a house just so we could have the basement all to ourselves.

"Andre decided to get even, so he tried to talk to my wife and Gary's. He met my man's girl somewhere, somehow and he booked her. They started doing their thing. The girl was kind of unhappy with my man Gary because he had her on lockdown and kept her in the house with the baby.

"So this kid Andre met her. Gary found out about it and he was furious. Being that I knew I was fucking Andre's girl, I decided to talk to him for Gary. My man Gary was ready to take him out because Andre knew that was my man Gary's baby mother and you don't do that, but I'm boning Andre's girl. Andre wasn't a tough guy or anything, he was about getting that dollar.

"I went to go talk to him, 'Yo, Andre check this out, me and you are doing business, the money is good, but you have to stop boning Gary's girl. Gary knows, he's upset and he is giving fair warning. He's letting this one go because he doesn't believe you all had sex and I don't even want to know, it's not worth it.'

"He was like, 'Yo, I hear you good looking out.' He told me this straight to my face. So about two or three weeks pass and Gary calls me again. He says, 'This kid Andre has to die. He's still seeing Caprice. This time I want to deal with him.'

"So Andre calls and says he has 270 g's to spend, I figure I can kill two birds with one stone. I could have the money and his girl. I called Gary and we met Andre. I pull up and get into the car with Andre, he gives me the money and Gary sneaks up and shoots him in the body, killing him.

"We dump the body, wipe our fingerprints out of the car and split the money. They found him like two days later from the smell of his body." Alpo was a coldblooded killer who didn't think twice about killing for money. Because remember with Alpo it was never personal, always business.

That murder ran through the rumor mill on the streets of the Chocolate City. Even Twala heard about it. "Dude was fucking with Gary's baby mother. Alpo was fucking dudes baby mother, so he felt like he could kill two birds with one stone. He was going to meet him for a transaction and he killed and robbed him. Got the money and kept the coke and jewelry."

Alpo was always scheming. He had a Machiavellian kind of flair. He moved pieces around like master chess players and if someone got in the way, Alpo terminated them. One of Alpo's victims was DC street legend Michael Fray.

"He was about to get back in position in DC. He had a list of names of people who he needed to eliminate and I was at the top of his list. I found out because I was feeding someone in his camp he wasn't taking care of. That same person in his camp ended up killing him for me," Alpo said.

But street lore holds that Fray had chumped Alpo for some kilos, multiple times, when Alpo first starting coming to DC and never paid him. So in reality the assassination was payback, street justice, gangland style. Alpo was the type of dude who couldn't take a slight to his ego. If you disrespected him in any way, he would get his revenge.

Alpo like the snake he was, even turned on one of his friends. He had done it before with Rich Porter and he would do it again. It was second nature to him. With all the murders what was one more Alpo figured. As long as he would benefit he was down with it. One of the bodies that grabbed the attention of homicide detectives was that of Alpo's main man Garrett "Gary" Terrell.

"Gary was a short guy about 5-foot-2 with a real slim body and a big head, people didn't know he was getting money, he had about $2 million in cash. He was getting it. He had a real Napoleon complex though. At one time we were really close. I knew his family and he knew mine. I knew where he laid his head at and he knew where I laid mine. I knew where his stashes where and he knew where mine were. He was also the one with me with Rich. We had a lot of secrets on one another." Alpo said.

"He became jealous of me because people used to see him with me all the time and I was Alpo. So they began to think he worked for me. It wasn't until I came to DC that he started to come out with Benzes. He saw what I was driving, so he started busting out with 300 coupes and all that.

"I always had a reputation though. If you let me hold your car it automatically became my car. So when they saw you driving your own car, people thought it was mine and you were driving it. When I couldn't get to my car I would drive Gary's. Then when they saw him driving it they thought it was mine. People didn't know he was getting it like that.

"We'd talk and he'd be like, 'People think I work for you.' Girls always thought he was a big head funny looking little boy. It just started to get to him. Time went on and one day we were in a restaurant with one of his workers and he called my wife a bitch. I just looked at him.

"I could have taken it better if we were alone, but he said it in front of one of his workers. I had love for Gary. I told him before this and a few other times things happened. 'We know too much about each other, if we were to ever get into any confusion or anything one of us would have to leave.'

"I was getting too much money, so I wasn't going back to New York. The only thing left is one of us would have to die. He was like 'I feel you.' I had this deal coming up with this connect. A big deal where they wanted me to put up $2 million for $6 million worth of coke. I was about to put the deal together in New York. I called and asked Gary if I put up $1.5 million did he want to put up the other half a mil. This would have put us on the map for good.

"It was 11 grand per key. I could have gotten 19 grand a key in DC easy, right before this, Gary and I stopped hanging out, but I wasn't really paying attention, I still had mad love for him. He ended up telling someone he was cool with in prison about the deal.

"What he didn't know was his man was cool with my man Wayne. I had never told Wayne about the deal. When Wayne told me about my deal I was like 'What the hell. How do you know?' He said his man said Gary told him about it. He said Gary was going to do me in the process.

"Wayne was ready to do him. I was like, 'We have to do it right. We can't run up to him in broad daylight. It would come back to us. We have to get him where no one knows.' At the time Gary had a little beef with these kids and they tried to kill him a month earlier. He beeped me one night and told me he knew where the kid Jawbreaker was. He was one of the kids trying to kill him. I asked Gary who he was with, he said he was alone. I asked him what he had on him. He was like two pistols.

"I was with Wayne and two other dudes who were under

Wayne. I made sure Gary was alone. This was our perfect opportunity to make it happen." Alpo was ready to kill his little man and he called in the dogs to help him get it done. Like a chess master Alpo always moved the pieces into the right positions, ensuring he would come out on top.

"From what I know is Alpo, Wayne, a guy named Tom Sales and Jerome was there. Tom Sales and Gary was in the back, Wayne was sitting in the front with Alpo. Supposedly they picked Gary up and Gary thought they were going to kill somebody else. Gary supposedly put a hit out on Wayne and he didn't know that Wayne knew and was tricking him into the car to be killed first," Twala said.

"We cruise around looking for this kid Jawbreaker." Alpo said. "We stall for time. At one point we thought the cops were going to pull us over so we put all the guns in the stash, including Gary's two. When the cop didn't pull us over I grab a revolver from the stash and give it to the kid who was sitting next to Gary I gave the signal to bang Gary in the head and they blasted him twice, two to the head. He never saw it coming.

"We left him near a telephone box. The telephone people came to fix that particular box the next day, that's how they found him." With the murder of one of Alpo's closest associates, the alphabet boys were onto him and Wayne. The killing of a known associate turned the heat up. There was just too much death around Alpo and Wayne. The feds were ready to put down a full court press.

"With friends like Alpo, who needs enemies," Velma Porter said. "He admitted to killing his friend Gary in a fashion unfit for the most profound enemies." Alpo didn't care, he proved that again and again. But his recklessness was about to be his demise. He thought he was untouchable, but his day of reckoning was coming.

In June of 1990, Nathaniel "Nut" Watkins, who was Rich Porter's first cousin, was arrested in Washington, DC with drugs and cash. He was charged as a kingpin. Authorities in New York were notified of Nut's arrest, because he was a known associate of Rich and Alpo. Agents went to DC to interview Nut, who was facing a sentence of 20 years to life in prison.

Upon meeting with Nut the agents explained how they would help him if he were willing to cooperate with the government. Nut agreed, he told the agents that he received drugs from Alpo and distributed them in DC. In Nut's mind, it was get back time. He would snitch on Alpo for his cousin Rich. But dudes make up all kinds of excuses and justifications when they snitch. That's how they make it ok in their mind.

"Rich's cousin Nathaniel told on me. Nut, as we used to call him, was dealing with Rich and there was a time I was getting some joints from Rich. One day Nut needed 125 grams for a Virginia customer and he got it from me." Alpo said. "Nut was another guy I almost killed back in the day for AZ.

"I did the old mobster shit to him. AZ was talking to him in the front seat. I was in the back. I just grabbed the seatbelt around his neck and started choking him. Nut's thing in Virginia goes down. Rich is dead, so when Nut wanted to talk to the feds they told him they didn't want to talk about Rich. So he told them I was his supplier. The feds put a warrant out on me. I'm on the run for the next two years."

FBI agents in Washington, DC joined the investigation. Alpo was on the run from the FBI for over a year. A CI told federal agents of Alpo's whereabouts and connected several unsolved murders in DC to Alpo. The loop was closing and this time it would be Alpo's neck it was wrapped around. Not a position he was accustomed to being in.

"I was putting together an indictment to tie Alpo into murders and giving him the death penalty," the U.S. Attorney said. "He gave orders, other people killed. Alpo was charged with drug conspiracy and money laundering. Later in a superseding indictment the FBI added five murders. Alpo was a major prize for the feds, a big man in the Harlem drug trade."

By 1992, Wayne Perry was in jail in Prince George's County, Maryland where he was being held on a number of charges. When he appeared in court to plead guilty to one count of selling a counterfeit substance to an undercover, he was arrested and charged with first degree murder for the October 23, 1991 slaying of Garrett "Gary" Terrell in furtherance of a continuing criminal enterprise.

"Where my man was located in Southwest was two blocks away from the federal building, they didn't know where I was. They kicked in my son's mothers and my mother's doors. So once they did that, I knew they didn't know where I lived. I wasn't really worried about them. I knew if I was in a car, they weren't catching me. I knew once they came once or twice they would just wait to see it someone would tell them," Alpo said.

"Prior to this I had already run from the feds when they were staking out one of my houses. I had a joint with an elevator in it. It was a three floor house with a two car garage, den and Jacuzzi on the third floor. I also had an apartment where I kept the coke two blocks from my house. I used to come from DC into Virginia for the coke. My apartment was only five minutes out of DC.

"If you called and said you wanted five joints I would come to Virginia. Everything was highway for me. With certain customers who I had a relationship with I would jump off the highway, pull up on the side of their car, throw them the drugs, they'd throw me the money and I was out. I just kept it moving. The apartment I had was in the same building where Monica Lewinsky lived. The Watergate Towers in Virginia.

"When I ran from the cops at my house, this guy told them where I lived and one night when I was coming home I was about to turn into my garage when I saw two white guys in a gray two door Celebrity. I knew it was the feds. They just wanted to know if I lived there. They thought I was there to stay. I was out of there. I had a 300ZX turbo. That day I got away."

It wasn't long before federal agents received info that Alpo was living in an apartment complex with his wife and after several days of stakeouts on November 7, 1992 they finally spotted him. On November 10, 1992, Alpo was arrested on cocaine distribution charges in Northern Virginia. He was also wanted for questioning in drug related killings from Washington, DC to New York. He was 25 years old.

When they arrested him they found drugs and money in the car. Alpo said little at his brief hearing, but sniffed loudly as he cried in court. The Harlem hustler knew he was in a jam. With the noose around his neck he was in a position he wasn't accustomed to. How will I get out of this, he must have been thinking as his cocaine dream turned into a nightmare.

PART 8

BETRAYAL

"I'm Alpo, before you snitch dog." Shyne, That's Gangsta Shyne (2000)

FBI Arrests Long Sought Drug Suspect, The Washington Post headline read on November 8, 1992. Alpo was arrested by the FBI and DC police as he drove his truck in Southeast Washington, near Pennsylvania and Minnesota Avenues. The feds finally got their man. They had their eye on him for a minute and they finally grabbed him.

"It was scary because I knew once they came for me it was over," Alpo said. "At the time I was waiting for my wife to pick me up. I was sitting in a car when this dude walked past the car. I grabbed my two nines. I put them back because he just kept walking, then disappeared. My wife pulls up, I get in her car to talk to her. As we drive off a car comes up behind us. Right across from where we were is an Amoco on Pennsylvania and Minnesota, where they had a police car waiting.

"I told my wife to pull over because the cops pulled us over. The ones that were at the Amoco. In my mind I'm saying I had

10 fake IDs and my wife has her license. No problem, we really didn't do anything. What I didn't know was the feds were behind it all the time. I wasn't paying attention.

"They told her to shut the car off and asked that the passenger step out. I just followed orders. When I stepped out they jumped out the trees and came running out of restaurants. All kinds of cars came from out of nowhere.

"I jump back in the car and my wife tried to throw the car in drive, but she never got it into drive, only neutral. The car just sat there revving real high. They snatched her out the window and threw me to the ground.

"One of the agents was like, 'Give us the famous smile.' I looked up and just smiled at them, they were like, 'Yeah, that's him.' All the pictures they had of me, I was smiling, plus they just wanted to be funny.

"When I went to the federal building they had a can of Alpo on the table. They gave a can of Alpo to the federal agent who finally got me. I'm thinking damn, this is serious. I've got to fight these people. I have to get my paper together. I called my lawyer. He came and represented me and my wife. They locked her up too, but she got out that day."

Dressed in a brown leather coat and jeans, Alpo appeared in court and waived extradition to Virginia. He knew what the deal was. He was indicted in July 1990 and knew he was a fugitive on the case where Nut had snitched on him. It was time to pay the piper and go to jail.

"I'm thinking I'm Alpo, I have to go out like a trooper." Alpo said. "They sent me over to DC jail. I hooked up with some dudes I used to deal with on the street. A few beefs tried to start because of Michael Fray.

"His nephew was in there with a couple of other dudes that rolled with him. I was a little too strong for them. Then my man Wayne sent word to me in the jail to make sure I was all right. The dudes in my unit were like, 'Don't worry about nothing.' I started getting familiar with certain guards. I even got some pussy.

"Then they sent me to Virginia for my original complaint, which was Nut, Rich's cousin. I was sitting in Alexandria Detention Center. Sitting for months not knowing what the hell is going on. My lawyers telling me they have you for this and that. I'm thinking I can fight this. This is nothing. I didn't do anything over here. I'm not thinking DC is coming. I'm thinking they have me for something in Virginia.

"What DC was doing was building their case. Once I was in jail other people were willing to come forward and testify against me. Other crews before me were going to trial and coming back with natural life. My lawyer was like you really need to make a decision. I was really trying to see if I could fight these people. I was going through all the preliminaries. The kind of evidence they had on me. I was trying to fight.

"My lawyer said, 'Your ace in the hole is if they even ask you to tell, you really need to think about that.' It wasn't until a year later that I decided to do that. They were busting people from my crew.

"This guy Dave, he's the one that told them where my house was. I had my boat, cars and houses in his name. They had a kid from the military who I used to get guns from. My lawyer came back at me and was like, 'Look they're trying to make a deal. They want you, but they really want Wayne.'" It wasn't a hard decision for Alpo. He had been betraying dudes all his life- Randy Love, Rich Porter, Gary- what was one more betrayal? Alpo had always made it clear; he always went for self when it came down to it. Not knocking him, just telling the truth.

"Wayne wasn't sure that Alpo was telling," Karen Garrison, Alpo's wife said, but others disagreed. "Wayne knew he was telling because they held him on a humble." Twala said. "Wayne kind of figured something wasn't right with the nigga. That's why Wayne said he was going to kill him. It didn't happen and niggas was like Wayne should have killed that nigga." But at first nobody knew for sure that Po had flipped.

"Po was so slick that he used them, he orchestrated the police to come and buy the murder weapons. Nobody knew that he was setting then up." The Uptown player says. "All these weapons and everybody's fingerprints on them. That nigga wasn't trying to go to jail. He was doing a lot of crazy shit in New York before all that DC stuff."

Alpo gave the government information on dozens of people from DC to New York. He said he never snitched on anyone from New York, but that was a lie. Alpo was doing him, plain and simple. He didn't give a fuck about anyone else or any kind of loyalty or the rules of the drug game. He was going all out for himself.

"He remembered everything in all this detail, he told the feds, let's negotiate a contract, Alpo was a businessman. He knew he had more info that he could trade. Alpo brought to the table that kind of businessman mentality. He never acted out of anger or animosity." Alpo's lawyer said.

Alpo made a calculated decision and snitched out his man Wayne Perry for a reduced sentence on the 14 homicides he pled guilty to. He was very Machiavellian in the way he went about it. He manipulated things on multiple levels, no one ever catching onto his game. He played dual roles, switching from gangster to informant, when ever it benefited him.

"First time they saw each other in about a year or two was at a hearing." Twala said. "Alpo was in a year prior to Wayne getting locked up. Wayne was in on another charge due to the fact that the government was building their case against him. Alpo was turning in states evidence at the time, but we didn't know.

"So we came to court and his bitch ass got on the stand and he was still trying to holler out stuff. If you could have seen the look on Wayne's face, it looked like he could kill Alpo with his eyes. It was a very tense moment. Alpo was a bitch and he didn't have no heart, Wayne had the heart."

The government's case against Wayne Perry rested on testimony from Alpo. Alpo pled guilty and admitted his involvement in a series of drug deal related murders and cooperated with police snitching on Wayne, Tyrone LaSalles Price and Michael Anthony Jackson. He turned on everyone he did business with in DC.

"The feds caught Alpo and he told on his killing team in order to spare an execution sentence," AZ said. He didn't cover up anything. He sold everyone out and put it out there that he did what he did. He was Alpo of course and would spin everything to make himself come out on top. Right or wrong, he did what he did, and wasn't afraid to admit it.

"I told it all," Alpo said. "Sometimes in the game it's either you or the person." That was Alpo's attitude. He was doing him. Fuck the code of the street. He knew when it came down to it, it was him or someone else and he chose the next man. So much for death before dishonor.

"They had the key witness, that was Alpo," Twala said. "The death penalty was originally for Po, but he shifted it onto Wayne. Wayne told me that this nigga is trying to get the racist muthafuckas to inject me."

Alpo was going all out, he didn't give a fuck what the streets or anybody thought. He was doing him. "Alpo snitched on his most prized confidant in DC, Wayne Perry. That must have ripped his soul apart more than any sentence that could have ever been imposed on him" Velma Porter said.

On March 5, 1993, federal prosecutors unsealed a 27-count indictment charging Wayne Perry, Tyrone Price and Michael Jackson with committing murder in the furtherance of a continual criminal enterprise for the execution of nine people; conspiracy to distribute crack cocaine; racketeering; conspiracy; retaliating against a witness; kidnapping and robbery. The indictment was based on the cooperation of Alpo, who had already pleaded guilty to

ordering multiple murders.

According to the indictment Perry, Price and Jackson were paid by Alpo for killings in drugs or money. From 1989 to 1991 Perry was involved in eight of the group's nine homicides. One was the July 17, 1990 shooting death of DC street legend Michael Fray Salters. Fray died because Wayne and Alpo learned of his plans to kill Alpo. Alpo and Wayne paid Michael Jackson nine grand cash, a half-kilo of cocaine and a 9mm handgun to kill Fray, court records indicated.

The drug operation allegedly shipped more than 500 kilograms of cocaine into DC, between 1989 and 1991. Wayne Perry was identified by law enforcement as the premiere shooter and hit man for the drug gang headed by Alpo. In June of 1993 the government decided to seek the death penalty against Wayne Perry in federal court. Prosecutors alleged Perry was responsible for killings for hire, torture, kidnapping and retaliation against witnesses.

"I went with the flow," Wayne said. "I don't fear nothing and no one." After a number of ups and downs, betrayals and double crossings, Wayne Perry pled guilty in US District Court to five counts of murder in furtherance of a continual criminal enterprise for the killings of Domenico Benson, who was shot as he was shaking Alpo's hand; Evelyn Carter, who was allegedly cooperating with police, she was shot in the head at close range leaving Constitution Hall; Yolanda Burley; Alveta Hopkins; and Garrett "Gary" Terrell.

Wayne was immediately sentenced to five life terms. In March of 1994 at the age of 31, Wayne Perry's run in the streets was over. He was feared in the streets and his respect level was on one million, but his legacy was cemented when he upheld the street code of no snitching and took his hit like a soldier and made man.

"I didn't cop out because of the death penalty. I live to die. I copped out to make sure others didn't get life. I took the bull by the horn to save others. That's the kind of man I am," Wayne said. "Make no mistake about it, Po is a spineless coward, a rat of the highest order.

"I will never understand how people praise and romanticize snitches, rats and sellouts. I would die a thousand deaths before I ever compromised my principles as a man. As I think back I always knew Po was weak and capable of everything he displayed. I had my reasons for not putting him in the dirt. I should have put the barrel in his mouth."

But Alpo told on Wayne before he could kill him. In reality, part of Wayne Perry's fame is that Alpo told on him. They were two vicious gangsters doing a deadly dance, a dance that either dictated life or death, and Alpo struck first. Had it not played out that way, Wayne would have surely ended up killing and robbing Alpo for all he was worth. And Alpo knew this, so he got Wayne the only way he could and saved himself in the process. Not justifying it, because Wayne wouldn't have went out like that, but lots of hustlers and stone cold killers in the game do. So let's keep it real.

PART 9

THE OUTCOME

"Niggas like chips to get it like Rich/I would've said Alpo, but that nigga's a snitch." Jim Jones

Alpo turned snitch at the same time the government was really cracking down on drugs. National policy was changing and the get tough on crime rhetoric was becoming popular. There were more cops on the streets, more prisons being built and the feds were waging the War on Drugs with mandatory minimums and the federal sentencing guidelines. The public was sick of the drug epidemic and the crack era gangsters with their gratuitous violence and get mine mentality changed the way the criminal justice system operated.

In New York City and Washington, DC, multiple agency law enforcement units were formed and went through and picked up everybody who was anybody and then some. Dudes were telling like never before and the code of the streets was only being upheld by the most thorough. These men have gone down in the chronicles of gangster lore. And then there is Alpo.

A lot of people blame Alpo for starting the whole snitching

trend, but that is far fetched. He was just someone who was looked on highly and admired greatly. He was a certified street legend and when he snitched, he severely tarnished his legacy. But regardless of his detractors, that legacy is celebrated in hip-hop and street lore.

"That took people back damn near in a state of shock when that nigga started telling." The East River boriqua says. "Nobody saw that coming, but experience has shown that selfish ass niggas, when caught up in a spot like that, will continue being selfish ass bitches and tell on everyone, so they can weasel their way out.

"Alpo would have went down in the streets as a living legend if he would have kept his mouth closed and just took his time. Instead he is remembered for being the flashiest rat out of Harlem. His mother still lives in 430, in East Rivers. His sister does not. His son's mother, Little Margie, was a beautiful girl, body and face. She lived in his building. Everybody went nuts for her. Their son's name is Gumby."

As the 1990s rolled around, the drug culture and hustle, lost its allure and was no longer a game that brought respect. With the tragedy of crack and the government's War on Drugs, it stopped being cool to be a drug dealer and popular culture decided that "crack was whack." Rappers like LL Cool J, romanticized the drug dealers and glorified their lifestyles in their videos. But the reality was all the real gangsters were sent off to prison, with multiple decades or life sentences.

In the midst of all this, Alpo was shipped off to federal prison. He was housed in the Bureau of Prison's Witsec program, which is a Witness protection program for those witnesses whose crimes dictated that they do some time. Alpo began serving his time for the 14 homicides he confessed to, including the murder of his best friend Rich Porter, in one of the BOP's cheese factories, as they are called. His location remained hidden, not known to the general public.

"I had to confess about everything for my deal," Alpo said. "Once you take the position I've taken, you have to tell it all. If there comes a time later on that they find out about something else, whatever agreement they gave, they could take me back to court. For the four murders in New York, I basically got immunity. They just added them to the murders in DC."

Just like he did in the streets, Alpo was going all out for self. He wasn't faking. He was being the best snitch he could be. Besides taking down his killing crew and other DC dealers, Alpo also gave information and assisted in getting Don Diva founder and Harlem street legend, Kevin Chiles, busted and indicted in 1994.

"Alpo set a dangerous precedent that should not be emulated in any regard. He tried to convince the masses that snitching is cool and passé. He called it, 'Doing Po.' I call it old fashion telling. Those that compromise their manhood by giving Alpo the time of day when he comes home will only testify to their own weakness," Velma Porter said.

"It is said that Wayne Perry was so hurt during his indictment that he didn't even try to deny the accusations because he couldn't believe the very man who he tried to keep alive at all costs was trying to kill him via a lengthy prison sentence."

Thanks to Alpo, people snitch and call it, "Doing them." They reason, "If Alpo did it, than it must be all right to do." That was how much sway and influence Alpo held in the streets. His infamy has outlived his run in the drug game and hip-hop culture still embraces him.

"I'm charged with 14 murders," Alpo said. "Eight in DC, two in Maryland and the rest in New York. I want to take this opportunity to clear two rumors. One is that I'm dying of AIDS in prison. This is false. I'm healthier than I have even been.

"The other is that Po is snitching. If that's what you want to call it. That's what you call it, but Po calls it looking out for Po. I'm doing what I have to do for me.

"Also, for the people who read this and say Po went out like a sucker, in life you make choices and sometimes those choices are good and sometimes they are bad. At the time, when I did what I did, I had to do it for me. In my time in prison, I have come to the decision that I truly made the right choice.

"There was a time I really regretted it, but in the years dealing with people and seeing how people treated me as far as coming to visit me and looking out for my family, I know I made the right choice.

"First off, the government wasn't dealing with me on a 10 or 20 year bid. They wanted to give me the death penalty or the rest of my natural life in jail. Unless you're facing that, don't judge me." The streets have judged Alpo and found him wanting.

"Wayne hates his ass," Twala said. "Wayne was a good dude to a lot of people. Wayne was a real gangster. Wayne was true to the game. He held his own in court." To the streets and in the annals of gangster lore that's how it is portrayed, but still dudes keep it real. Defending Alpo to the last.

"The dude Po is a rat and I am not elevating his monkey ass, but he did some things other so called hustlers of New York didn't have the nuts to do then and still don't now. Real talk." The Spanish Harlem hustler says. "What fucks me up is that now due to the fact that Po is a snitch, the same niggas talking shit know they were scared to death of him. I'm not talking about Wayne Perry or Boy George. The rest of these muthafuckas act as if Alpo won't gun them down now. The Preacher is a snitch too, but he is still a killer."

Alpo has been buried in the Witsec program in the BOP for over 20 years now. Trying to work that sentence down so he could get out sooner. But there was never any doubt that he was getting out. And Alpo being Alpo, he played the part no matter what dudes thought of him or how he was perceived.

"He really thought he was like that," a dude who was in the Witsec program with Alpo said. "He bragged about what he did, what he took from cats, real scumbag. He was always trying to work shit to get a time cut. He still had many followers in the streets who tried to build cases to help him."

In the Witsec units Alpo interacted with all the high profile snitches. "Alpo treated dudes differently depending on who they were," the Witsec prisoner said. "Clowns he would clown, the respected ones he gave them respect, but he stayed in dumb shit. I think he was kicked out of every witness unit for all types of dumb shit.

"Doing interviews, smuggling shit in, talking about other inmates on the phone, a real no, no. But he knew just what not to do to get kicked all the way out of the program. So he bounced from unit to unit. Last I heard he was in FCI Otisville in New York."

Dudes on the Witsec units got to each other good. The Witsec units were small units with not many people and everybody was high profile. Strong opinions were formed concerning Alpo, but nothing was said to his face. "Alpo was an idiot with no remorse for anything, cold blooded, too dumb to hustle. He was a class clown, just all over the board, loved to talk about what he took from dudes more than anything." The Witsec prisoner said.

"He hung out, talked shit, stayed on the phone when he could, some C/O's would let you make social calls on the legal phone, guys could ride for three or four hours. Not just Alpo. These places were wide open. One C/O for 80 to 100 guys, so you could do whatever really." As Alpo did Po in the federal Witsec protection program, his legend in the streets grew.

PART 10

STREET FAME

"Yo, black is flashy like Alpo/gun happy like Pappy/ picture this young nigga/getting' it like Rich Porter." 50 Cent, 50 Bars of Pleasure, Guess Who's Back (2002)

The streets have welcomed Alpo's legend and his name has remained relevant, despite his snitching. His exploits have graced the big screen, magazine covers, books, documentaries and rappers rhymes. He has gone down in the chronicles of gangster and hip-hop's lyrical lore as an icon that influenced popular culture.

"Me, Rich and Po were getting mad money real young. We was ahead of our time." AZ said. "We bought jewelry, cars and houses like most people bought socks. We had love in the hood and we helped other people to eat. Even music industry cats started copying our style and shouting us out in songs. We got cats hustlin' and flossin' like we did."

The movie Paid in Full was centered on Rich Porter's life and produced by Damon Dash and Roc-A-Fella Records, but Cam'ron as Alpo clearly stole the show. His early rise to fame in

Harlem is portrayed in the film. And the 2002 American crime drama, whose title was taken from a 1987 Eric B and Rakim song, took in 3 million at the box office. But when Paid in Full came out, AZ wasn't happy with it. He wanted the movie to be a cautionary tale, not one that celebrated the lifestyle.

"I gave this man a powerful screenplay," AZ said of producer Damon Dash. "But now it seems more like a marketing plan to promote his rappers. Plus Cam'ron is too rah-rah about the drug game. I never chilled with Cam'ron too much, but I must say he portrayed Alpo well. Paid in Full encourages people to idolize the game and its star players. Alpo, who caused a lot of death and destruction is glamorized and portrayed as some sort of street hero."

Cam'ron, Damon Dash and Jim Jones- they have all paid homage to Alpo. Cam'ron was the spitting image of Alpo in the movie. It seemed he wanted to be Alpo. That he idolized Alpo. His rap persona was based on Alpo. "People like Dame Dash idolize Alpo and therefore made a movie about him. Still others obviously envied him and couldn't wait for his fall from grace to deride him. To me, he was nothing special, so I don't see why his name keeps popping up." The Harlem gangster says.

"The more people talk about him, the more important he appears. Maybe that's the plan, so the late bloomers can finally get some shine. The only relevance some people seem to have is directly related to their relationship with others, whether positive or negative." The film came about as AZ hustled the trio's story.

"I never seen Damon Dash before, but he said he did business with Rich and heard about my screenplay and was interested, he said you will be straight for life after this," AZ said.

"It was a good film and I love Damon Dash for making it happen. I was on set a couple of times, but since Rich and Alpo weren't there, I felt I had to let them do them. It was a good movie. All I got was 100 g's cash. Patricia Porter got something and I think Alpo got something.

"It wasn't broken down into one piece, it was broken down into four years. I spoke to Alpo twice since he has been locked up. That was when I was trying to do the film and he agreed to send some papers. We spoke again during the Kay Slay interview." Alpo was in the Witsec program living big, talking about his entertainment dreams since his cocaine dreams were dead.

"He was a real tool. Loved to talk about his infamy. Just couldn't shut up." The Witsec prisoner said. "Always had his folder full of articles, mags, anything he didn't like of course was not true. He was always speaking about the Rich Porter stuff and how AZ fucked him over with Roc-A-Fella, Jay-Z and Dame Dash and the movie shit. I guess AZ took less money, so they quit talking to Po."

In Po's world everything was always someone else's fault. "I tried reaching out to AZ, but he's been phone ducking me. I didn't think he was going there, but I should have looked at the whole time he's been ducking me. He got the kid Damon Dash under another impression, like he's been looking out for me or something. They were hitting AZ off with $10,000 or so every four months." Alpo said.

AZ also did a F.E.D.S. magazine interview around the same time, which Alpo didn't like. "The whole thing with AZ and his F.E.D.S. magazine interview was I didn't appreciate the way he portrayed me to be some type of flunky." Alpo said.

"As far as Rich is concerned, AZ was trying to glorify the dead. Don't get me wrong Rich was a good person, but he had his bad side too. Let's talk about how he killed his best friend's brother because they were selling crack in front of one of his spots on 132nd Street. Let's keep it real if we're going to tell the truth. I knew both sides, because I was in with Rich and I was in with AZ. I know AZ didn't like Rich and Rich didn't like AZ."

AZ pushed the story about the trio. It was his claim to fame. Since he was out of the game, he was pushing the story hard, trying to get book, movie and DVD deals. He was on the street networking. He even had a rap group that rapped about Rich's legacy in the streets.

"Troy Reed wanted to come out with a magazine first, but at the same time F.E.D.S approached me about a story." AZ said.

"So I was like Troy you do the documentary and let them do the magazine. Everything sparked from there, F.E.D.S. magazine was born and Street Stars DVDs was born. Troy Reed is like the Spike Lee of street docudramas"

After AZ spoke his piece in F.E.D.S., Alpo responded in a lengthy F.E.D.S. magazine interview. He told dudes in the Witsec unit that he got paid $7,500 for the interview. The AZ and Alpo stories and interviews put the street magazine genre on the map nationally as F.E.D.S. and the market blew up.

"F.E.D.S. is a magazine that features the stories about street hustlers and urban crime." AZ said. "Many of its biggest supporters are on lockdown in this country's prisons. In the late 1990s, F.E.D.S. magazine interviewed me. They wanted me to reflect on the drug game and my role in it. That was the first issue of F.E.D.S. and I' sure my article helped the magazine sell like hotcakes. The next thing I know, F.E.D.S. released an issue in which Alpo granted an exclusive interview from prison."

The streets and Harlem were obsessed with Alpo. He launched the career of DJ Kay Slay and the entire street magazine genre is indebted to him, because Alpo catapulted the original street magazine F.E.D.S. into the market place by being on the cover. His legend and legacy far outstripped his real actions, taking on a life of their own.

"The F.E.D.S. magazine came out with Alpo, Rich Porter and everybody on it and everybody in the hood was going crazy." The rapper Cam'ron said. "These guys had furs on, they had jewelry, they were flashing money. I'm looking at it like I got 10 furs in my closet, I got mad jewelry. I'm bugging. This is what people want? Let's do it. If you look at the whole Diplomats Volume 1, I just jacked the F.E.D.S. thing."

It's evident that Alpo and Rich Porter heavily influenced street culture and hip-hop with their flashy and fast paced lifestyles. The story of Alpo, Rich and AZ was told in F.E.D.S., The Source, The Village Voice and a number of other periodicals. The photos on the cover of the F.E.D.S. issue were taken at Darryl Barnes birthday party; it was him, Rich and Alpo.

"I talked to them because they talk the language of the streets. F.E.D.S. is on the inside looking out. Everyone else who writes about us is on the outside looking in." Alpo said. The street mag was accepted by prisoners and hip-hop alike, along with Don Diva, its rival, very quickly.

F.E.D.S. magazine, largely due on Alpo's interview, became a sensation in the prison system and quickly gained 7000 subscribers in prison. The magazine became a media darling. Street Tales, Grisly and Raw; Grim True Crime Magazine Hits Home with Inmates, The New York Times headline read on December 5, 1999. Criminal confessions and tales from the dark side of hip-hop life were a staple of F.E.D.S. It billed itself as the magazine for convicted hustlers, street thugs, fashion, sports, music and film.

"I want to show the other side of this life," Antoine Clark, the magazine's publisher said. "I want to show what happens to these gangsters when things go wrong, as they almost always do. I wanted to show what was real, what was going on. I've seen these people get killed, one after the other. I know how these big time criminals in prison cry at Christmas and at night because they are alone. It seemed time to tell about real life and tell about it in the language people use."

By tapping into street culture and the criminal lifestyle and world, F.E.D.S. grew to a 30,000 press run which cost $81,000 to produce for the 72 page magazine. It has always been the publisher's contention that the magazine doesn't glorify crime. But just as hip-hop offers a look at the criminal and gangster underworld three minutes at a time, the street magazines spawned an industry that celebrated street legends like Rich Porter and Alpo.

They have been the subject of many documentaries and Don Diva covered the Rich Porter story in their article Hell up in Harlem in issue #5. Rich Porter's mom even spoke on Alpo's interview in F.E.D.S. All the voices from this story have been heard except Rich Porter's, and his voice will never be heard but his legend lives on.

"I am deeply saddened by the manner in which Alpo portrayed my son, when in fact in his heart he knew what he said was untrue. It is easy to try and vilify the dead, when the dead has no advocate to counter claims against them. My son's spirit cries out from his shallow grave." Velma said.

"Alpo has chosen the narrow path of shifting animosity and disdain on others to dim the lights of some of his most atrocious crimes against the ones that loved him the most." The outcry from Harlem has remained strong against Alpo, but it hasn't diminished his street star status, only enhanced it.

AZ formed a rap group called Mobstyle and released a hit song in Harlem about Richard Porter that represented the era. He also went on to pen a book called Game Over and did the Troy Reed documentary of the same title. On his album, AZ raps about street life and the tragic kidnapping of Rich's littler brother.

"Mobstyle is the music, Paid in Full is the movie and Game Over is the book." AZ said. "I released the book Game Over, it's the most serious book on the streets. The street bible on some real shit and written by me, to try to warn people about the game and give them the heads up on what's going on. Its about the life of AZ, Alpo and Rich Porter."

Game Over, the documentary, was narrated by JadaKiss and came out in 2002. "Game Over was very successful thanks in large part to Pat Porter," AZ said. "Pat warns young brothers about getting involved in a game where there are no real friends, no real love and no real honor. It was difficult for her to recall those painful memories. But she refused to let her pain get in the way of speaking the truth.

"The beginning of Game Over focuses on me, Rich and Alpo. However, I did not want my documentary to glamorize the cars, money and women. I wanted people to see how cold and deadly the drug game is." Troy Reed's Street Stars put out another documentary on Alpo called The Alpo Story. Both DVDs gained critical acclaim and their success led to BET's American Gangster series and other documentaries.

A lot of Harlem and Bronx rappers- Cardin, Jim Jones, Juelz Santana, French Montana, Shells- they all rap about Alpo and pay homage to him. Jim Jones and Cam'ron are supposedly shopping a sequel to Paid in Full that is based exclusively on Alpo's life. The story of Alpo and Rich Porter have made a lot of people a lot of money. Jim Jones even got a deal with Timberland to put out "the Ghost of Rich Porter" boots that retail for $175.00.

"I hope people can see one day that we didn't do this because we wanted to. Circumstances and images shaped our reality into wanting to be a hustler," AZ said. "You can't stop it. That's like trying to take a bone from a vicious hungry dog. They have to eat. If you don't have another way for them to eat, what you're saying is obsolete.

"All I can do is give them little jewels to keep their heads up on the game. Such as look for the door instead of looking to stay in this forever. Set it up were you're going to make this amount of money and then you're going to stop." Smart words from the man whose life was nearly snuffed out by the dangers and treachery of the drug game. But he has already achieved the fame that many men crave and he knows the temptations of the life intimately. As does Alpo, who has become the most popular of the trio.

A lot of real gangsters and stand up men are sick and tired of Alpo getting his 15 minutes of fame and then some. They probably won't even like the fact that this book is coming out in the Street Legends series. But whatever dudes think, Alpo is a street legend. His name is still relevant 25 years later. But still everyone is entitled to their opinion. That's what makes the world go around.

"I'm not defending Alpo, its just I think people like him are so insignificant to the grand scheme of things. How many times do we have to hear about this small-time drug dealer/middleman/rat and his showtime gangster pals?" The Uptown player says. "My issue with that rat Alpo was for crossing me, along with making himself out to be some sort of true player." But the truth is a lot of dudes have problems with Alpo, because his name is still relevant.

Being a legendary figure in hip-hop's lyrical lore makes Alpo relevant and keeps his name popping up in popular culture. The truth of the matter is that Rich Porter, AZ and Alpo were legends in their own time. They lived it, they flaunted it, they owned it. On DJ Kay Slay's The Truth, LL Cool J rapped, A seventeen year reign, simple and plain/when I ruled the rap game and all my peers sold cocaine/1-3-2 uptown, when Rich Porter told me/"See you can push a new car, it's different for a rap star/ and AZ was giving 50s to the homeless/they never bragged about it: "L, we don't condone this."

Alpo was recently released from the federal Bureau of Prisons Witsec program. After almost 26 years its said he came home in December and is rumored to be living in Atlanta in the Witness Protection Program but only for six months when he will make his arrival back into the world public. It's said he has many supporters in the hip-hop industry waiting to embrace him when he does. "When I come home, I'm still gonna be king." Alpo said. And AZ recently released two more documentary's on Rich Porter, can an Alpo bio-pic be forthcoming?

The life and times of Alpo and Rich Porter have gone down in infamy in the chronicles of gangster lore. Everybody from the crack era in 1980s Harlem is either dead or in prison doing life. All the big names that were celebrated in Harlem have either been killed, served lengthy prison terms or been affected negatively by the drug game in some way. So even though it seemed like all these dudes won, in retrospect they lost.

"Darryl Barnes is in a wheelchair, Doo Wop is in prison. LA and Rich are dead," the Harlem gangster says. The huge Harlem machine of drug lords that AZ, Alpo and Rich Porter championed finally collapsed, and no one picked up the scepter, except to glorify the life in rap lyrics. The crack era is long gone, but its impact has reverberated and hundreds of thousands are paying the price for the vicious exploits of all those legendary crack era gangsters and gun thugs.

"Alpo may have put fear in most, but real men saw him for who he really was- a no good, double crossing parrot who tried to walk in Rich Porter's regal shadow and could never quite attain the grandeur that he attained." Velma said. "Alpo's son will grow up knowing that, through his own words, he is the biggest rat and disloyal friend that has ever walked the streets."

AZ probably summed up the whole episode the best. "When Alpo killed Rich, he not only killed Rich, he killed Harlem." That is the prevailing sentiment, but the legends live on. The cocaine dreams of Alpo and Rich Porter have influenced many rappers and entertainment figures. And at the same time inspired many youngsters to try and follow in their footsteps and become street stars in their own right.

SOURCES

The New York Times
Don Diva Magazine
Wikipedia
Faces Magazine
F.E.D.S. Magazine
Panache Report
freewebs.com
How to Hustle and Win by Supreme Understanding
nymag.com
sherdog.net
Amazon.com
As Is Magazine
The Washington Post
gorillaconvict.com
Raised By Wolves by Cavario H.
Asphalt Gods by Vincent M. Mallozzi
The Source Magazine
The Streets of Harlem by Lester Marrow
Street Legends Vol. 1 by Seth Ferranti
Street Legends Vol. 2 by Seth Ferranti
Game Over, Street Stars DVD
The Alpo Story, Street Stars DVD
4Front Magazine
Vibe Magazine
Stop Smiling Magazine
Game Over by Azie Faison
I Make My Own Rules by LL Cool J

ABOUT THE AUTHOR

Seth Ferranti is a multi-media writer and journalist who pens amazing true crime and prison related stories for vice.com and thefix.com among others. He started his career in journalism while incarcerated and is now continuing it in the real world. In 1993, after spending two years as a top-15 fugitive on the US Marshal's most wanted list, he was captured and sentenced to 304 months under the federal sentencing guidelines for an LSD Kingpin conviction and committed to the custody of the Attorney General.

A first-time, non-violent offender, Ferranti served 21 years of his 25-year mandatory minimum sentence. His case was widely covered by The Washington Post and Washington Times, and his story was profiled in the pages of Rolling Stone and Don Diva magazine. He is currently working out of St. Louis, Missouri. During his incarceration Ferranti worked to better himself by making preparations for his eventual release back into society. Ferranti earned an AA degree from Penn State, a BA degree from the University of Iowa and an MA from California State University, Dominguez Hills through correspondence courses.

He is now ready for all that life offers. It appears there is no stopping him. Seth also writes for thedailybeast.com , substance.com, hoop365.com, Don Diva and F.E.D.S. magazines and The New York Daily News. You can order his books on urban gangsters and prison life on Amazon.com or at gorillaconvict.com.

He also has a blog on that site that has tons of content on life inside the belly of the beast, prison and street gangs, hip-hop and hustling, the mafia and crack era gangsters.

Made in the USA
San Bernardino, CA
18 April 2015